Contemporary International Theory
and the Behaviour of States

JOSEPH FRANKEL

Contemporary International Theory and the Behaviour of States

OXFORD UNIVERSITY PRESS
London   Oxford   New York
1973

Oxford University Press

OXFORD LONDON NEW YORK
GLASGOW TORONTO MELBOURNE WELLINGTON
CAPE TOWN IBADAN NAIROBI DAR ES SALAAM LUSAKA ADDIS ABABA
DELHI BOMBAY CALCUTTA MADRAS KARACHI LAHORE DACCA
KUALA LUMPUR SINGAPORE HONG KONG TOKYO

PRINTED IN GREAT BRITAIN BY
RICHARD CLAY (THE CHAUCER PRESS), LTD
BUNGAY, SUFFOLK

'... One should not expect an apple-tree to produce cherries—one should judge it by the quality of its apples. A man without practical experience as a policy-maker or as an adviser to policy-makers is unlikely to contribute much by usurping a role for which he is unqualified; his best chance of being useful lies precisely in the realms of academic analysis.'

STANLEY HOFFMAN

Preface

THE aim of this book is to introduce the reader to theoretical ways of thinking about international relations rather than to expound the details of the various approaches; it concerns itself with what theory is for and about, rather than what it actually is. Moreover, it is selective in its emphasis, concentrating heavily upon the behavioural approaches and, within them, upon the role of values and the concept of the 'national interest'. This emphasis is somewhat idiosyncratic but it enables the author to devote maximum attention to a field in which he has most expertise and also to apply the theory to concrete examples. The various approaches and concepts are illustrated by examples drawn mainly from post-war British foreign policy.

The analysis excludes purely theoretical, more abstract points and mathematical formulations and concentrates upon the aspects of theory likely to shed some direct light upon state behaviour.

Chapters I–II introduce the reader to the general aspects of international theory; chapters III–VI analyse the major three groups of approaches; chapter VII is a case-study. A brief glossary of basic concepts is appended.

I would like to thank Mr. Ian Rennie who helped me with part of the research, to my colleagues Mr. David Thomas and Mr. John Simpson for reading the draft and making some useful suggestions and, most of all, to my wife for her assistance in editing the final draft.

J. F.

May 1972

Contents

List of Diagrams

For permission to include diagrams we wish to thank The Macmillan Company of New York (Diagram II (© 1971)) and Prentice-Hall, Inc. (Diagram IV (© 1968))

List of Diagrams

1
Theory and Practice

_____

1. INTRODUCTORY

THE social roles of the practising diplomat and of the academic theoretician of International Relations are, of course, entirely different. Although Political Scientists were frequently interested in influencing political activities throughout history (cf. Plato) in the classical, rationalist doctrine of political theory, the distinction between the theoretician and the practitioner was clearly made. Thus de Tocqueville stated: [1]

The first [aspect of politics] is based on the very nature of man. It depends on his interests, faculties, and needs and is revealed by philosophy and history, his instincts changing their purpose at different times, but without changing their nature, being as immortal as the human race. This aspect of politics shows us those laws best adapted to the general and enduring state of mankind. All this is science.

Then there is also a practical and militant aspect of politics coping with everyday problems and adapting itself to a multitude of varying circumstances. It provides for the passing needs and is aided by the ephemeral passions of its contemporaries. This is the art of government.

Of course art and government are different, and practice does not always follow theory.

There is always a link between theory and practice: theory distils the basic principles of practice and, by providing 'metapolitics', influences it in turn, although generally with a considerable time lag. In our generation, however, this time lag has disappeared and the science and the art of politics seem to converge again, particularly in the United States. In a circular process, many theoreticians become increasingly eager to learn about the obscure governmental processes directly from the practitioners and, some-times, also to exercise some influence upon these processes, whereas the practitioners increasingly feel the need of outside assistance with the increasingly complex problems of our age.

De Tocqueville's remarks however still apply and relations between the two remain, as they have always been, uneasy and distant.[2] The common concern in this field is shared and both sides are fully aware of the potential value of their mutual rela-tions but they are divided by basic differences in attitudes and orientations, they belong to different subcultures now further divided by problems of the 'scientific' jargon. The theoreticians are fundamentally concerned with their theories and with their controversies about them, however irrelevant these often are to the practitioner. They are often critical of governmental policies, not always for theoretical reasons alone; 'the pursuit of truth' can disguise savage ideological warfare, well exemplified in the stand of the majority of the United States academic community on American involvement in Vietnam.

Although there are many critics of the government among the academics, there are few martyrs among them.[3] Many of them co-operate—because they are attracted by the possibilities of find-ing out otherwise obscure facts, of wielding power, and, last but not least, of receiving funds for research. Nevertheless, the two sides view each other with suspicion. Whereas some members of the academic community who wish to intensify contacts complain about the drying up of governmental funds, others complain about the dangers of ideological contamination[4] and the abandon-ment of the search for truth. The practitioners operate without a clear conception of basic research and are concerned only with 'relevance' for their current tasks. No institutional expedients of integrating theory and practice have proved successful—whether the farming out of research projects, or the establishment of 'independent' government-financed research institutions, or trans-fers of personnel. Although a recent conference of theoreticians and practitioners favoured the growth of research and planning departments within the central departments of state, nobody was very confident about the outcome. As one participant wittily described the practitioners' view of the scholar in a scenario of 'functional social engineering' in international relations in the year 2001: 'Predictably, one of the committee members complains plaintively, "we ask these social scientists what the time is, and they give a history of Swiss watchmaking".'[5]

As other participants commented, it remains unlikely that the President would seek the advice of a peace research specialist before going to a peace conference meeting and the prospects of an international relations research yearbook for the practitioner are extremely remote. Nevertheless, however difficult, perhaps impossible the *application* of the research appears to be, everybody seems to be acutely aware of the importance of its *implications*. In fact, is the situation fundamentally different from that in natural sciences between 'pure' research and Research and Development? Even more precisely, it is possible to divide thinking about International Relations into basic, strategic, and tactical, as the Dainton Report did in 1971 in its analysis of the relationship between the various branches of the natural sciences. The limitations of this analogy are, however, considerable. First, it is extremely difficult to find the links between basic and applied political science and, second, there is as yet very little of the tactical science (e.g. theories of decision-making or of bargaining) whereas in natural sciences the applied part is colossal and is of great tactical relevance.

Of course the American experience is not necessarily germane for Britain. Nevertheless, here, as in the United States, some of the diplomats[6] and the theoreticians are now increasingly baffled by the complex and intractable reality they are dealing with, dissatisfied with the adequacy of their respective activities, and subject to outside criticisms about them; perhaps often also subject to similar temptations to avoid facing squarely their respective problems by finding some reasonably honourable escape. Probably the major use of theory for the practitioner lies in broadening his approach by an appreciation of long-term interests and of the relevance of the international system which is the environment for our foreign policy. These could be gleaned more easily not from the theoretical literature directly concentrating upon them but rather from the applied studies of state behaviour: unfortunately, the latter are still extremely rare.

2. PROBLEMS OF DIPLOMACY

In the majority of the theoretical approaches the diplomats are placed squarely within the decision-making apparatus which operates within the domestic environment and, for foreign policy purposes, mediates between this environment and the international one; diplomacy serves as an 'interface' between the two environments. This, apparently, corresponds with the diplomats' own perception.

If some theoreticians accuse diplomacy of being inadequate for its contemporary tasks, this criticism, it seems to me, stems largely from the traditional, rather narrow, assessment of their role by the diplomats themselves and the much broader definition by the outsiders. Two aspects of traditional diplomacy are frequently singled out for criticism:

(1) insufficient appreciation of the fact that changing the perceptions of others may be a more promising method of exercising influence than the development and application of one's own capabilities; a parallel concentration upon inter-state disputes[7] which results in a relative neglect of the rapidly growing cooperative tasks;

(2) the increasing inability of the diplomat to control or even coordinate other channels of inter-state interaction, both governmental and non-governmental, which are rapidly reducing the relevance of diplomatic activities.

Both criticisms are likely to appear as unjustified to the diplomat. Surely diplomacy has always included alliances. Moreover, the craft is traditionally interpreted as being a mere instrumentality, as being governed by the foreign policy decided upon by the 'political masters' and as being subject to the imperious constraints of the international environment. This is, however, the position of the diplomat as it is generally seen and indicated, although often only indirectly, in most theoretical approaches.

The domestic environment

The differences in the definition of the role of diplomacy apply particularly in relation to the domestic environment. It is a truism that the constitutional theory of the Civil Servants serving, as their name indicates, their political masters is only partially true. We know, of course, that the Prime Minister or the Cabinet can decide upon a policy which does not command the support of the Service[8] but the point surely is that these disagreements are rare and that normally the political decisions are based upon the advice of the diplomats although, to some extent, this advice generally anticipates policies likely to be acceptable to the political masters.

Closely allied is the relationship between diplomacy and the substance of foreign policy. Far from being restricted to a purely subordinate and executant role, to most outsiders, diplomacy seems to be closely intertwined with the formulation of foreign policy, especially through such subtle matters as the choice of emphasis and the presentation of possible alternatives in the advice tendered. If the diplomats claim and presumably often believe that they merely execute a foreign policy decided by others, this often means that this policy has not been openly debated and sometimes that no policy decision has been taken at all.

Diplomatic advice to the politicians may quite frequently concern itself with the domestic interests involved but it is, by definition, primarily concerned with the foreign policy aspects. The constitutional myth is that such interests would be known to the politicians and would be duly represented at the Cabinet or at least at the Parliamentary level. In fact, domestic–foreign linkages are so difficult to comprehend that even the theoreticians specializing in them are still very hazy about them.[9] Domestic pressures seem to reach the highest political level only rarely, when they lead to the organization of pressure groups (e.g. the Katanga Lobby) or to a massive, electorally relevant public opinion movement (e.g. opposition to rearmament in the thirties). Undoubtedly governmental autonomy is much higher in the United Kingdom than in the United States and hence the 'model' of governmental decisions being the product of internal bargaining[10] is less appropriate. Nevertheless, if essential domestic 'inputs' are not taken *fully* into account in the original diplomatic scrutiny of the issue, rectification at the political level would be much more difficult and, failing sufficient pressures, is unlikely to take place. For example, in a recent issue, was there a suitable *diplomatic* procedure to study, to take into account, and to include in the briefs the intricate possibilities of a strong turn of public opinion against Britain's entry in the E.E.C.? Arguably the Foreign and Commonwealth Office is better left with the more limited task of analysing the international considerations as the domestic ones would not be ignored by the Cabinet and would merely confuse their brief and obstruct rational proposals. The ultimate choice of priorities is political and must rest in the hands of the Cabinet.

Closely connected is the political vacuum with respect of fundamental considerations of basic values and of the 'national interest'. Presumably on all new issues, the Civil Service advice roughs out an appreciation of the 'national interest' involved, which would be independent of party politics. The Civil Service must, however, also anticipate the likely interpretation of the national interest by the Government in power and, once policy has been decided, they must keep within the decided brief. Thus, without being able to contribute much, they become involved in foreign policy decisions which appear to be taken without a clear consideration of the broader issues of the national interest, although these are so frequently invoked by the politicians, or in decisions taken for narrowly partisan party reasons.

Outsiders tend to blame many of these shortcomings upon the diplomats. Obviously diplomatic activities could not be readily broadened to cope with them and it is not suggested that diplomatic advice could be altered accordingly. Could it, however, perhaps with assistance from theory, help to plug the important gaps mentioned by attending more to the central values and to other domestic considerations?

The international environment

Here the problems come squarely within the traditional scope of diplomacy and have been recently discussed in the Duncan Report.[11] Two areas of problems are well identified:

(1) The flow of information and its interpretation are hampered by excess of marginally relevant items; this is a field well explored by the social communication approach.
(2) Foreign policy activities by other agencies urgently require co-ordination.

A third problem is less clear and more intractable—how diplomacy which, despite its experience in alliance politics, is essentially geared to competitive or conflicting interaction can be geared to co-operation, especially to ensuring a more desirable international system rather than a position of advantage and influence within the existing one.

3. USES OF THEORY

If it is accepted that a broader conception of diplomacy may somewhat reduce its present problems and limitations, theory can be quite useful to it, both for intellectual and for political reasons.

The bulk of this argument is concerned with intellectual reasons, i.e. how, despite all its shortcomings which are duly noted, even at this early stage of its evolution, the theory of International Relations can provide interesting new insights and angles. There is also, however, an important possible *political* use of theory, i.e. as a convenient and often quite convincing explanation of why diplomats should broaden their traditionally limited briefs and introduce broader considerations which they feel are relevant, such as those pertaining to the domestic environment or to the national interest, or involving suitable generalizations and comparisons with other States. It is, for instance, much more telling to explain the reasons why Britain should or should not do a thing not only in terms of the issue itself but also by relating it to the country's power status (cf. in the records of the Duncan Report, 'a major Power of the second order'), or comparing it with what a state of a similar status (say France) is doing in a comparable situation.

In this respect theory would be used for legitimization; it would be a rationalization rather than the reason for broader interpretations. This would not be a cynical or Machiavellian use of theory; it is merely a prudential, pragmatic one, enabling the diplomats to get done those things that they want to be done. If theoretical arguments are unlikely to play a major role in the acceptance of diplomatic moves by the political masters or public opinion at home, they may become increasingly important in their acceptance abroad, particularly in relations with the United States whose diplomats are being trained in international theory and are likely to employ its concepts to greater degree in the future. They may play a crucial role in the context of the E.E.C. in deciding between conflicting national interests: a British diplomat there, even if he does not employ the 'integration' terminology, could easily prove vulnerable to arguments of others which are couched in it.

Returning to the intellectual uses of theory, the following are suggested in the relevant literature:

(a) *A general broadening effect can be expected.* To draw from a related field, Roberta Wohlstetter argues[12] that 'a willingness to play with material from different angles and in the context of unpopular, as well as popular, hypotheses is an essential ingredient in a good detective, whether the end is the solution of a crime or an intelligent estimate'. The advantage of non-confirming advice is generally recognized in all political systems. Particularly instructive (though by no means transplantable to Britain) was the Kennedy experiment described by Robert Neustadt in *Presidential Powers* which aimed at creating conflicts among the presidential advisers to ensure a broader selection of alternatives. Such broader choices seem essential in periods of rapid change when the organizational tendency both of the Diplomatic Service and of the Government and the State as a whole obstruct rapid adaptation.[13]

The impact of international theory upon the U.S. Government has been significant. The American analysts have helped the governing bodies to perceive the historical world in a certain manner, just as Keynes had taught them to view the economic world from a certain angle. This perception does evolve from the conceptual system, from the elaboration of models (first strike, second strike, counterforce, counter-cities strategy), and from certain propositions that common sense suggests (for example, the disproportion between the cost of any nuclear war and its eventual gains). This strategic view of the historical world inspired the leaders of the United States with a doctrine that tolerates limited warfare (with the use of conventional weapons only), recommends the control of armaments with implicit (and sometimes explicit) understandings between the two Nuclear Powers, and reduces the risks of a total nuclear war to a minimum. The result—a doctrine probably sensible, but not rationally administered.

(b) Systematic, if you wish 'scientific', thinking is introduced; better definition and organization of concepts enables us to manipulate them with greater ease. For example, an account of a diplomatic issue from the 'decision-making' angle may not substantially diverge from or add to a common-sense account written by a historian or a practising diplomat. Nevertheless, starting with a general analytical framework, it has the advantage of posing questions some of which might not otherwise be asked, and of arranging the account in a way which could be used much more readily for purposes of comparison. More specifically, theory helps us to organize the storage of data, their classification and their retrieval, their meaningful organization with the help of political concepts, the search for additional data, and the articulation of our assumptions and prejudices. Ideally at least, it enables us also to proceed with greater clarity in identifying our relevant values and, ultimately, in determining the most rational course of action.

(c) Theory helps to separate and identify more clearly the relevant factors of an issue. This is particularly helpful when the issue has to be later considered in contexts different from the original one.

(d) As shown in economics, the tendency for abstract theory to become completely divorced from social reality does not prevent the development of an applied social science which combines a fairly rigorous theory with the consideration of actual reality.

(e) Like all social theories, international theory is capable of producing what John Stuart Mill terms 'mid-term theories', i.e. reasonably adequate explanations for a given point of time and place although the explanatory power of these theories rapidly diminishes when they are applied to different periods and systems. Thus the 'balance of power' theory was a reasonably adequate explanation of the basis of the nineteenth-century international system, as Marx's theory was applicable to the early stages of the Industrial Revolution; neither theory is able to explain later periods.

(f) Although unable to establish valid causal relationships, international theory has begun to establish well-documented and plausible correlations. Cf. the relationship between the incidence of alliances and the involvement in violent armed conflict for which a positive correlation has been established for this century but a negative one for the last century.[14]

(g) As the international system becomes increasingly integrated, some of the problems faced by States in similar circumstances are likely increasingly to resemble one another while the utility of their individual national traditions is likely to diminish. Hence the growing importance of learning from others through the use of analogies or paradigms. The former relate to specific previous experiences, either one's own or those of others; the latter postulate a basic similarity warranting a general drawing of comparisons. Diplomats, of course, use analogies very frequently, although often subconsciously and hence a theoretical clarification of what is involved should be of great interest to them.

In essence the operation is fairly similar and simple. Regarding analogies, the basic theoretical operation consists of specifying as precisely as possible the nature of the characteristic in respect of which the analogy is being drawn and hence the scope of the analogy; obviously a mistaken analogy can be extremely misleading and harmful. This introduces the need for clear classification—for example, Britain can be regarded as a Middle Power, a Western European State, an ex-Colonial State, an anti-Communist State, etc. Plausible analogies can be drawn from the behaviour of other States belonging to the same categories as Britain, but clearly only in respect of the shared characteristic.

The use of a paradigm, a yardstick for comparison and evaluation is often subconsciously resorted to when evaluation is difficult. *Prima facie* a State is likely to imitate successful and powerful States or those which are roughly similar. Clarification of what is involved would obviously be useful; thus, in retrospect, it seems fairly clear that in the early postwar years Britain followed the United States in many aspects of her external relations—foreign, defence, and economic, although, of course she diverged in other aspects. In some ways, Germany, Japan, and, to some extent, probably also France, looked up to Britain. The attitudes have now changed and characteristically the Duncan Report, admittedly only in an appendix and regarding the fairly technical problem of the reasonable size of diplomatic missions, refers to Germany and France as suitable yardsticks: likewise, for some time we have given up the unattainable goal of emulating the United States in advanced weapons systems. The role of theory in establishing the necessary classification is identical to that in drawing analogies.

4. LIMITATIONS OF THEORY

(*a*) Full causal explanation of the complex of international phenomena is impossible but many attempts are made to reduce them to one overriding principle (e.g. power politics, ideology, imperialism, or class struggle, etc.) and to produce a 'theory' around it. Even with explanations which assume the more modest form of a hypothesis or a hunch rather than a fully fledged theory, we are only too frequently wrong—cf. the widespread Western belief that propensity to violent conflicts is connected with autocratic political systems which has been invalidated by detailed research, or the Communist counterpart correlating it with ideological clashes which has been invalidated by the Sino-Soviet and the many other inter-Communist conflicts.

(*b*) Searching for precision and certainty easily leads people to desperate efforts to force the variety of social life into the mould of 'scientific' theories. In the words of George Lukacs, 'there is this desperate urge to do the "scientific" thing which is a hangover from the nineteenth century and reflects the inferiority complex of the social scientist'. Social scientists are not immune from analogies as far-fetched as that attributed to a famous physicist who was said to contend that entropy was nature's way of atoning for original sin.[15]

International theory, like other social sciences is preoccupied with methodology and devotes much more effort to improving methods than to reaching substantive results—the contributors themselves and their critics tend to judge results by methodological prowess even if the substantive results are insignificant or banal. In a way, this preoccupation is natural in view of the bewildering results of the two related facts that, in principle, human beings appear to have freedom of choice and also that they are activated by their own systems of interpretation and sets of beliefs about the social world. Consequently, however, a large part of international theory tends to concentrate upon minor and not particularly relevant matters because these are the only ones for which we can develop reasonably adequate tools of investigation. The contention that the tools thus sharpened will be available for attacking major, more intractable issues is not fully convincing.

Methodological obsession is a frequent besetting sin. As neatly put by a leading philosophical theoretician, Morton Kaplan, the theoretician can often be likened to a person given a hammer to whom everything becomes a nail. A special, rather important sub-category is obsession with quantification which leads readily to the neglect of central issues because they are not quantifiable.

(c) In its legitimate and fully understandable search for 'scientific precision' international theory goes to excessive lengths in attempting to redefine political concepts which, on the whole, are used loosely and vaguely. This inevitably leads to the accumulation of conflicting and confusing definitions and to the employment of excessive numbers of newly coined terms, resulting in a jargon which is sometimes scarcely understandable to those not versed in the theory, however much they may be interested in the field of international policies. Occam's Razor is insufficiently applied. Nevertheless, a degree of agreement could be and, in the fullness of time, is likely to be achieved within the profession which will eliminate at least some of the excesses.

At the same time, some new concepts are useful and necessary. For instance that of a 'penetrated political system' advanced in the 'linkage approach' which will be discussed later, is used to denote politics in which foreign agents participate in the decisions made within them. To a large extent this concept coincides with that of 'imperialism' but is much more sharply defined and lacks emotional overtones, and hence it is much more useful.

(d) Analysis tends to become ahistorical, i.e. to concentrate upon the manipulation of a few selected variables which are highlighted by the given approach in a manner increasingly removed from reality. Owing to the simplifications of reality inevitable in the assumptions made by the theoreticians, this happens even within the much more limited field of economics. Obviously in the broader political field the simplifications are even more remote from real life and hence theory tends to become even more esoteric.

Closely linked is the limitation due to the way in which theoreticians put the emphasis upon regularities and ignore unique features. This readily lends to platitudes which, as Stanley Hoffman put it, are often an excellent point of departure, but always an execrable destination.

(e) Although the accusation is sometimes unfairly made that the models employed are confused with reality by the writers, it is in fact rather hard to avoid the temptation to oversimplify reality in order to produce elegant and cogent models.

(f) The predictive powers of theory are limited to specified sets of assumptions. This resembles economic predictions similarly based on the formula 'if so ... then' with the additional limitation that the assumptions in international theory are even less realistic and hence predictions even less dependable.[16]

(g) An intensive controversy continues over the mode of analysis of international politics despite the fact that there is a fair degree of agreement about its substance. Both major opposing camps, 'the traditionalists' and the 'scientists' are divided among themselves. Thus in a recent volume[17] devoted to the controversy, we find complete confusion in the evaluation of the work done. For example, Hedley Bull criticizes Morton Kaplan for espousing but not practising the scientific method; Kaplan willingly accepts this distinction; but Marion Levy regards it as inaccurate on the grounds that Kaplan does not seem to comprehend the science he is espousing. It is extremely difficult to persuade other theoreticians to agree to any one approach or terminology. Although the activities of the various schools have been linked to an 'unruly flock of activies' and the adherents of each school, at least at the lower levels, often operate in a kind of 'intellectual jail', by the later sixties the controversies somewhat abated and the scholars stopped stressing the differences among them and began to concentrate upon the similarity and the complementary nature of their approaches. Nevertheless, the speed and abundance of theoretical work continues to confuse, as new methodologies proliferate and few attempts are made to build upon the work already done. There is thus a dual division, not only between theory and methodology in general but also between individual theories and methodologies.

(h) The fragmentation of theory results in large and crucial areas of social life remaining unexplored. Social scientists dealing with International Relations are prone, like their counterparts in other fields, to work on the basis of their assumptions and constants, leaving their investigation to an 'unseen colleague' who does not really exist. A striking example is provided by our ignorance of the working of international economics: both the economists and the political scientists work on the 'unseen colleague' assumption. Thus, even when they are willing to resort to some form of rational decision-making through relying upon 'expert' advice, the politicians are left free to follow their hunches and prejudices and always find some theory available as a rationalization.

Looking at the divisions of theory according to the classes of people pursuing them, it is possible to distinguish five separate categories:

(1) Theoretically-minded politicians—Lenin or Hitler.

(2) Policy-oriented and theory-minded diplomats, e.g. George Kennan.

(3) Policy-oriented theoreticians in a receptive political context like Herman Kahn or Henry Kissinger.

(4) Policy-oriented theoreticians in unreceptive conditions—the peace researchers except perhaps in Sweden.

(5) Abstract theoreticians who are not concerned with the application of their theories at all.

2
The Nature of International Theory

1. THEORIES, MODELS, AND TAXONOMIES

IN the authoritative statement of the pioneer of the international theory, Professor Quincy Wright,[1] 'A *general* theory means a *comprehensive,* comprehensible, *coherent,* and *self-correcting body of knowledge,* the *prediction,* the *evaluation,* and the *control of relations among states* and of the *condition of the world.*' Consequently, to be precise, the word 'theory' should be used in inverted commas throughout this book—nothing which could be regarded as a fully articulated general international theory exists. The term 'theory' is used in a bewildering confusion with the looser concepts of 'conceptualizations', conceptual frameworks, 'analytical approaches', 'models', 'pre-theories', and many similar expressions. Not one of the so-called 'theories' resembles the tight logical organization or approaches the canons of verification (or rather falsification tests) of the theories in natural sciences; the academic community is nowhere near a consensus about the validity or correctness of any one theory, such a consensus being, in the informed view of Sir Peter Medawar, the operational hallmark of a valid theory in the natural sciences. All that 'theory' denotes is a general tendency to be analytical and to aim at precision and logical coherence.

In order to avoid using 'theory' as a misnomer, the application of the looser concept of 'model' seems advisable.[2] What a model means is a simplification of reality which need not answer the stringent criteria of a theory but is merely judged by our convenience—whether it helps us to organize the field and enables us to tackle to our satisfaction its major problems. Whereas a theory claims to be correct and hence excludes the validity of rival theories, a model is merely a convenient way of looking at things from a specific angle; the former can be considered as 'true' provided it cannot be falsified, the latter can be merely regarded as convenient or useful. To repeat the point, a model is merely a way of structuring the field which enables us to formulate hypotheses with regard to the characteristics around which it centres but does not aspire to an explanation. An important advantage of using models is that we are both able to systematize and to clarify our approach and are in no way precluded from using alternative models from looking at things from other specific angles, thus bringing into prominence all other elements which seem to us relevant. To illustrate this, perhaps somewhat abstruse distinction, the 'theory' of power politics, even in its cautious construction by Hans Morgenthau, is unconvincing as it does not satisfactorily explain the whole of State behaviour; a 'model' of power politics, however, is an essential approach to all inter-state relations as power obviously plays an important part in them. If we think in terms of a model alone, instead of trying to force difficult instances of State behaviour into the mould of our theory, we reserve them for scrutiny based upon alternative models, for example, that of social communication. Likewise, instead of joining the age-long controversy between the 'power political' and the 'ideological' theories of Soviet behaviour, it seems much more convenient to use a power political *and* an ideological model and to apply both of them in separate operations to a given instance of Soviet behaviour as well as to Soviet foreign policy as a whole.

The use of models helps to clarify our thinking but should not be pushed too far. Thus it is of dubious value as the basis for negotiations. These may be more profitably approached by establishing a set of certain firm criteria and engaging in an exercise of mutual mind-probing than by approaching the table with a set of cut-and-dried proposals deduced from the model as their amendment would be very difficult, if at all possible.

Before, however, attempting to develop models and theories, we face the preliminary task of classifying the phenomena we are studying into categories and classes. Adequate taxonomies are an essential precondition for effective theorizing. It is, for example, clear that we are likely to be much more successful in generalizations about State behaviour if, instead of thinking about all the States together, we confine ourselves to clearly defined classes of states: big and small, powerful and weak, rich and poor, according to their geographical location or ideological regime, etc., etc. The definition of criteria for taxonomic purposes frequently presents us with complex theoretical problems, e.g. how to define power or wealth. Hence the taxonomies we start with are, on the whole, fairly crude until we have advanced with our theorizing based upon them which, in a circular way, can then be put to use to refine our definitions of classes.

2. THE EVOLUTION OF THEORY

The theoreticians are in fair agreement that International Relations is a field of inquiry rather than a discipline.[3] The study has developed in what Professor K. W. Deutsch has termed four 'waves of advance' defined by changing approaches. Earliest in the field were the international lawyers who, for a long time, enjoyed a monopoly there. A second wave came through diplomatic history stimulated by the opening of many governmental archives in the aftermath of World War I and through interest in international organizations stimulated by the League of Nations experience. In the third wave, the scholars assimilated a number of relevant methods and findings from other social and behavioural sciences, especially psychology and social anthropology and also sociology. While this wave is still continuing, it is becoming reinforced by a fourth postwar wave—the rise of analytical and quantitative research concepts and of comparative methods. Striking formulations in this wave have been made through 'importations' from economics, mathematics, and systems analysis, and in a generally far-fetched way, also from ethology. Other writers distinguish phases of predominantly normative, empirical, and behavioural quantitative approaches or the progression from utopian, through realist, to behaviouralist and now post-behaviouralist analysis. All agree that the major problem facing the theoreticians is how to agree upon the selection of approaches relevant to our problems and how to synthesize them.

While the approaches are changing, the foci of interest are changing, too. Concern with States before World War I gave way to the interwar concern with the international system and the ways of improving it through the evolution of international law and international organizations. Since World War II, an undiminished interest in the international system is coupled with renewed interest in the behaviour of States and their interaction, which are now generally regarded as more amenable to analysis (and also to reform) than the system as a whole. In the study of State behaviour, in the postwar period attention has rather strongly swung from conflict to co-operation and, a parallel with it, from major crisis decisions to continuous, non-crisis behaviour. In the last decade, the focus has also shifted from 'capabilities' to 'intentions'. While the latter are now studied largely through psychological approaches which concentrate upon 'images' and 'threat perceptions', as well as by historical methods concerned with previous instances of State behaviour, possibly the next advance will be in the philosophical analysis of the values involved, the importance of which is at the moment acknowledged but not properly analysed.[4]

Hopefully, again, the majority of the new theoreticians regard their approaches as interdisciplinary or multidisciplinary. In fact, most of them are brought up in and based upon departments of political science. Few scholars in other disciplines have been giving major attention to International Relations although their technical expertise is being widely utilized. There are some outstanding exceptions such as Anatol Rapoport, a mathematician, or Thomas Schelling and Kenneth Boulding, economists, who have made fundamental contributions to theory. In general, the greatest contribution has been made by psychologists who have been studying attitudes to war and related matters since the 1930s and who started the research into 'tensions' in the 1940s. The misguided attempts at a general theory of war based upon the 'aggressive instinct' of man have, however, now been generally abandoned, and although all theoreticians, in varying degrees, accept the important role that psychological factors play in State behaviour, the very possibility of a general psychological theory of international relations is now denied.[5] The sociologists have shown relatively little interest in International Relations with the notable exception of Raymond Aron and Johan Galtung. The economists, with the already noted exceptions of Schelling and Boulding, became 'desiccated' in the 1920s through their attempt to eliminate psychology from economics whereas psychology of motivations and incentives lies at the very centre of both political practice and political analysis.

The present methodological trends have been thus summed up by Chadwick F. Alger:[6]

(1) The replacement of theory based on single, overriding causes with more complex theory. Furthermore, there is a recent trend towards the use of multivariate causal models, supplementing the correlational models that dominated research in the early 1960s.
(2) More systematic collection of data, both by advances in data-processing technology and by application of methodology from other social sciences.
(3) Utilization of the full range of available social science data-gathering techniques in international relations research, including observation, interview, aggregate data analysis, content analysis, and experimentation.
(4) Development of a historical perspective in more systematic international relations research through greater utilization of trend analysis.
(5) Application of theory from all the social sciences, particularly political science, sociology, and psychology, to the study of international relations.
(6) Development of an interdisciplinary community, primarily of political scientists, sociologists, and psychologists, by those who have stimulated the above trends.

In the present stage of its evolution, international theory is engaged in an extremely costly, laborious, and slow process of accumulating data which do not, so far, clearly fit into any plausible general framework. Such a pursuit, within its present scope, is clearly beyond the resources of academic communities outside the United States; this is not unmitigated disaster as, even among the American academics, some are greatly concerned with the use of the escalating mounds of data which may be limiting the vision of political life as a whole. There is also an excess of speculation; concern with political life as it is impeded by concentration upon how it might be. Scenarios such as those produced by Herman Kahn or Bernard Brodie can be, of course, useful for policies and by encouraging them to think about alternative forms of world order, but they are not a guide to reality.[7]

3. THE PRESENT STATE OF THEORY

The bewildering variety of contending approaches, the lack of substantive advances, and the difficulties of application to concrete foreign policy problems, all contributed to a growing concern with 'the crisis of relevance' of international theory; intellectual dissatisfaction was strongly reinforced by the concern for future financing among the many American academics directly dependent upon the continuing flow of lavish resources from the Government.

In recent years the confidence has, however, revived, despite the slow drying up of governmental funds, and many leading American scholars are increasingly stressing the interrelationships and intellectual affinities rather than the confusion and the untidy overlap between the various approaches. Many contributors, particularly those who are somewhat unsure of themselves, remain interested in proving their uniqueness rather than in studying their similarities with others and acknowledging their intellectual debts. As this manifests itself in many publications, it seems well worth concentrating upon the interrelatedness of the various approaches.

The hallmark of all theory is an attempt to view events and issues not in isolation but as parts of larger patterns of international interaction. Details may, of course, be hotly disputed, but I very much doubt whether any theoretician would seriously question the validity of the diagram on p. 21 which shows a simplified scheme of interaction between two States as a basic representation of international theory. Without any difficulty, except that of somewhat greater graphic complexity, this diagram can be broadened to represent foreign policy as a whole, presenting it as interaction with a number of states, international organizations, and the international system as a whole.

The various approaches concentrate upon different elements of the diagram but their operation is, on the whole, similar: they analyse in great detail the element they study while they 'blackbox' the other elements. This implies reliance, without much further questioning, upon findings of other approaches. Since unfortunately, we are far from unanimity as to what findings should be generally accepted, we are sometimes not quite sure about the exact meaning of the blackbox elements.

The basic split in international theory is between the 'tradition-alists' and the 'frontiersmen' or 'behaviourists'. The former claim that the new contributions have little, if anything, to add to the traditional lore of political science, history, and law and that the pretentiousness of their 'scientific' methods and of their mathematical formulation disguises a paucity of creative thought. The latter, some of whom are quite modest about their actual achievements, affirm that the only possible advance lies in the injection

DIAGRAM I. The interaction between two states

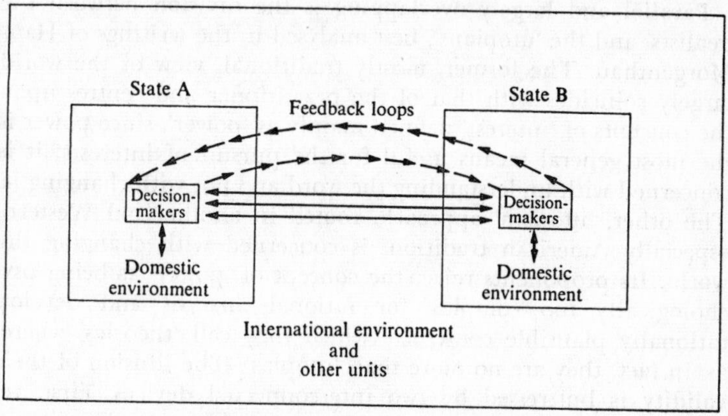

of precision, of scientific rigour, in the collection of adequate data, and in the development and improvement of new methods. In a way this is a fundamental epistemological question about what is researchable in some systematic, explicit way. On the one hand, if, as the traditionalists claim, we are faced in all decisions with decisive elements of uncertainty, contingency, and accident, the contributions of theory could not be important. If, on the other hand, as the behaviourists claim, we are only in an early, 'pre-scientific' period of international theory, we cannot as yet decide what sort of questions are really knowable or unknowable; our knowledge is determined not only by the nature of reality but also by the state of our intellectual apparatus, and we cannot as yet be sure how much the latter could be improved. In the above-mentioned discussion of this topic at the recent meeting of American scholars[8] the participants referred to the Cuban Missile Crisis in which the experience of seasoned diplomats like Chip Bohlen obviously carried most weight but some general theoretical appraisal of crisis behaviour could have been useful. To turn to a British case, could not the diplomatic experience in the relations with the E.E.C. and France be usefully supplemented by some general insight into integration and bargaining theories which will be discussed later? Moreover, could not the latter supply some arguments for the debate with the European partners which could conceivably carry some weight as being 'scientific' and therefore difficult to dismiss as special pleadings?

Parallel and largely overlapping is the division between the 'realists' and the 'utopians', best analysed in the writings of Hans Morgenthau. The former, mostly traditional, view of the world largely coincides with that of the practitioner and centres upon the concepts of 'interest' defined mainly as 'power', since power is the most general means useful for the pursuit of interests; it is concerned with understanding the word and not with changing it. The other, 'utopian' approach, rooted in another old Western, especially American tradition, is concerned with changing the world. Its proponents reject the concept of 'power' as being psychologically too complex for rational analysis and develop rationally plausible constructs which they call 'theories' whereas, in fact, they are no more than 'utopias'. The illusion of their validity is buttressed by two interconnected devices. First, reductionism: '... it is only by abstracting from that quality in politics, domestic and international, that resists pervasive rationalisation and is responsible for the moral dilemmas, political risks, and intellectual uncertainties inherent in politics, that it is possible to construct a morally and intellectually satisfying scheme. That distinctive quality in politics is the struggle of power.'

Second, quantification, based mainly on economic analysis: 'In such theoretical themes, nations confront each other not as living historic entities with all their complexities but as rational abstractions, after the model of "economic man", playing games of military and diplomatic chess according to a rational calculus that exists nowhere except in the theoretician's mind.'[9]

The contemporary approaches to international theory may be subsumed under the following broad headings:

The most abstruse of all is what may be termed *theory of theories* which is concerned with the basic ontological and epistomological problems. This cannot be clearly delimited from political philosophy and philosophy of knowledge in general.

Systems analysis is focusing either upon the international system as a whole or on the State as a unit operating within this system. In both cases it applies the methods of the general systems theory. Closely allied are the *social communication* or *cybernetical* approach which stresses not only systems but also processes of communication and of control and the integration and functional schools. Recent additions belong to the 'linkage approach' which analyses the links between domestic and foreign policies.

Theories of State behaviour concentrate upon single States. Within them the basic decision-making approach focuses upon the inner boxes of the diagram on p. 21, i.e. upon the decision-makers within the State. Other more traditional approaches concentrate upon capabilities, or institutions. Newer schools are concerned with images, or the 'cognitive' aspects of the decision-making process; and upon values, goals, and the national interest, or the 'volitional' aspects.

Interaction theory is concerned with generalizations about the 'patterns' of interaction. It includes conflict analysis as well as analysis of its co-operative alternatives. Especially relevant for the diplomat are the theories of games and of international bargaining as these are new ways of approaching the interstate negotiations which are the traditional major function of diplomacy.

4. METHOD-ORIENTED APPROACHES

It is possible to distinguish also a number of *method-oriented* approaches such as simulation, data-gathering, quantification, or prediction which can be applied in any of the groups. This introduces additional difficulties into a neat classification of the whole field which, even without them, is not very satisfactory, as to some extent the various classes overlap. Thus there is no clear division-line between State behaviour and State interaction and the late Arnold Wolfers thought of a two-angled theory which would combine them both; integration theory is a sub-branch of systems analysis but, at the same time, refers to State interaction, etc., etc. The major substantive approaches will be discussed in subsequent chapters, and the remainder of the present one is devoted to a brief account of the four major method-orientated approaches—data-gathering, quantification, simulation, and pre-diction.

Data-gathering. Following a spate of data-gathering activities in other branches of politics—especially on the characteristics of élites, mass opinion polls, electoral statistics, and various aspects of human attitudes and behaviour—some international theoreti-cians have made great efforts to establish reliable and strictly comparable cross-national data, which, despite all the United Nations statistics, is an extremely time-consuming exercise. The two major massive compendia have been produced by the Massa-chusetts Institute of Technology and Yale University.[10] The data collected are aggregative, mainly social, economic, and demo-graphic statistics, census data, etc., all of which are profusely avail-able from governmental, private, and international organization sources.

Whereas the major efforts are devoted to recent decades, re-search is also carried out on data related to previous periods with the aim of constructing time series and of studying historical trends. Other historical data consist of lists of historical events such as the well-known early lists of wars compiled by Lewis F. Richardson and by Quincy Wright.[11]

The scholars engaged in this field apply sophisticated methods in their work because, in the words of David Singer, the over-whelming unassorted accumulation of facts and of information requires systematic screening and codification by procedures which are visible, consistent, and replicable. Only then can we significantly use and compare our items of information; instead of being called 'data-gathering', the operation can be described as 'data-making' from the raw factual and statistical material.[12]

The aims of the workers in the field are ambitious. In the opti-mistic evaluation of a pioneer of these methods, Karl W. Deutsch, for example, we may learn more about and thus be able to test theories of inequality such as one produced by Gunnar Myrdal, once the distribution 'profiles' of seventy-five politically relevant variables already available *for* the States are matched with similar distribution 'profiles' of many of these variables *within* the States. We may learn more about the role of the individual States as equalizers or as promoters and stabilizers of inequality. Statistically more complex are the time series in which we can interpolate data for missing dates. Here the ultimate aspiration is a standard notation. This would include a 'trend line' which measures the central statistical tendency of the time series and the 'standard deviation' which measures the scatter of variance of the actual cases around this trend; with the secular trend, cyclical changes as well as the interplay of the random factors (the 'stochastic process') could be distinguished.

Of course we could, as some scholars note, become sadly 'data-bound' first by limiting our vision to political life as it is—not as it might be—and second, through the inadequacies of our language for theory-building and the relatively slow development of mathematical methods. One way out is through an extensive use of the computer. A striking example of what is possible is the basic operation undertaken by Russet in the quoted *World Handbook* in which a computation of correlations for each pair of set variables selected as salient in a given collection of countries, units, or cases produced about 2,800 correlations of which all those of 20 per cent or higher were printed out by the computer.

Another way out is the evolution of methods for a systematic construction of alternative futures. With increasing data and improving techniques, we can now make multivariate analyses of alternative hypotheses. The crystal-gazing may have limited or no predictive value, but makes us aware of the range of possibilities and prevents us projecting into the future some inflexible constructions based upon our data.[14]

Quantification. Closely allied with the former approach is quantification, as quantitative methods which are used in data-processing are also being increasingly used in other types of research. Here the profession remains split and the members employing the traditional methods stress the importance of 'the crucial intangibles' which are often overlooked by the quantifier who is engrossed in his methods and whose vision is accordingly narrowed. These 'crucial intangibles' may not be quantifiable at all in a way meaningful for the decision-makers—e.g. when it comes to the determination of the intentions of a major hostile State, no hard data produce a substitute for 'political wisdom' and we have not and cannot evolve reliable methods of judging the other side's intentions. According, however, to the leading quantifier, David Singer, 'there is no phenomenon of interest to the social scientist that is not, in principle, quantifiable'.

In fact the disagreement is not as fundamental as it sounds;

even traditional researchers often employ some quantitative methods and most quantifiers are well aware of the limitations of their methods. Moreover, the disagreement is, to some extent, a matter of semantics, of what we mean by 'quantification'. In a popular concept 'quantification' refers to figures, such as population counts or the size of Gross National Product; technically it is applied to all attempts to introduce hard data even at a low level of precision, e.g. by simple ranking (higher/lower).[15] At the same time, it is hard to conceive of a useful quantification of the basic elements of national purpose, e.g. President Kennedy's concern to avoid a flabbiness of national fibre which, among other considerations, led to the race to the moon. It would be extremely difficult to choose appropriate dimensions to compare in a quantitative manner the Labour 1945 purpose (to build a Welfare State?) and the Conservative 1970 purpose (to restore as far as possible individual enterprise and responsibility?) and their implications for foreign policy; it would be equally, if not more difficult, to compare quantitatively the French and British national purposes as they have evolved since the last World War.

In connection with quantification, increased use is made of mathematical methods, borrowing mainly from social statistics, economics, psychology, and also from pure mathematics. Most of the more sophisticated papers appear in the *Journal of Conflict Resolution* and the *Journal of Peace Research*. Much of the output relates to the theory of games.

In theory, the process of quantification appear to be simple. Any willing specialist can deal quantitatively with such factors as élites, their composition, coherence, and ideology; the capabilities of States; reactions to international and domestic inputs, etc., etc. On the basis of gradually built-up techniques, we can compare our forecasts with real results when they occur, and thus refine our methods. The experiences of the macro-economists should, however, serve as a warning. Doubts have recently arisen among them about the validity of the measurements they employ, especially for comparative purposes. Even with such standard concepts as 'Gross National Product', conclusions are often dubious, e.g. the relatively rapid growth of the French G.N.P. in the sixties is now justifiably attributed in part to a previously not recognised factor: a massive shift of peasants to cities meant that industrial wages which are fully included in the calculations of the G.N.P.

has been substituted for agrarian income which involves a large element for non-quantifiable subsistence economy production.

Mathematical models have severe limitations. First, they are based upon fixed assumptions and present closed systems whereas there seems to be much more promise in open systems which try to explain political behaviour without such fixed assumptions. Second, although the assumptions have to be made clear, it is often possible to disguise prejudices more effectively by mathematical symbols than by words; this is clearly the case with a large body of economic theory. Third, mathematical presentation confers a phoney aura of 'scientific' accuracy upon the argument and thus obstructs its critical assessment. For instance such exhaustive categorization of political systems as 'democratic' and 'non-democratic' or 'totalitarian' and 'non-totalitarian' according to precisely specified criteria would satisfy all the mathematical requirements of a nominal scale; in fact, any such specification would be based upon a simplification which may distort rather than enhance our understanding if its nature is disguised through the use of figures. Characteristically, much of the highly quantified theory relates to the 'cold war' and the nuclear balance where a fair amount of thinking can be done in rather simplistic military terms. Undoubtedly mathematical methods will be increasingly used in international theory as in all the other social sciences but the non-mathematicians generally share the view that the results hitherto achieved have not been particularly promising. It is indicative of the rather slow progress we have made that the leading recent reader on international theory includes only two items on the use of mathematics—a convincing one based upon the fairly old classical model of arms races by Lewis Fry Richardson which for a long time had passed unnoticed, and another, much less convincing one, on the structure of influence relationships in the international system.[16]

Simulation generally means 'an operating representation of reality'.[17] The inspiration for this technique has come from two sources; one technical, like the wind tunnel or the flight simulator, the other, the traditional military 'war games' which, in recent decades, have inspired also 'business games'. The delimination between simulation and games is a matter of dispute among the practitioners. The mathematical purists claim that simulation is something much more exact, in which all variables and relationships are explicitly and sharply defined and controlled and which is run through a set of mathematical equations or is operated by a computer. Most of the practitioners, however, extend the name to any exercise using players in a controlled environment. Over the last two decades the technique has become very popular in the United States and has also been employed, rather sporadically, in the United Kingdom, especially at the University College of Wales at Aberystwyth, at the Centre of Conflict Research, University College of London, at the University of Southampton, and also in several other universities. As no significant innovations have been introduced in the United Kingdom, I shall concentrate on the original American concepts.[18]

American simulation can be broken up into three major schools. To start with the least complex one, which closely resembles the traditional military games, The Political–Military Exercise, operated by Dr. Lincoln Bloomfield and his associates at M.I.T., consists of a small number, generally five, teams playing real-world nations, interacting within a well-defined situation and dealing with definite conflicts and antagonists. The game is controlled by a control group which plays the role of the international and domestic environments and feeds into the game the appropriate consequences of the behaviour of the players.

The Inter-National Simulation, evolved by Dr. Harold Guetzkow at Northwestern University, is more highly structured, as the teams, five to nine, representing nations, operate with sets of programmed variables; thus the participants interact in a more structured way than in the previous type of simulation because the domestic parameters of the decision-making process are programmed into the play. This is a mixed, man–machine type of simulation which has been used in many permutations, often without the computer. It has evolved interesting concepts dealing with domestic influences upon foreign policy behaviour such as 'decision-latitude' and 'validators'.

Most ambitious are the all-computer simulations well exemplified by TEMPER (Technological, Economic, Military, and Political Evaluation Routine) developed under the direction of the National Military Command System Support Center of the Defense Communication Agency for the Joint War Games Agency. Up to thirty-nine units represent real-world nations or groups of nations, each described by some thirty characteristics. The play quantitatively simulates international conflict situations and evaluates the roles of the various political, economic, cultural, and military factors involved. Problems are recognized and reacted to, leading to interaction which can develop into a variety of conflict situations similar to those in the real world.

The major drawback of all simulation lies in the relationship between the simulation and the 'real' or 'referent' world. Naturally the simulation world simplifies and therefore, to some extent, distorts reality. The distortion varies according to how much precision the operators aspire to; on the whole, the man-game, being relatively loosely structured, is also most realistic whereas the fully structured all-computer simulation is strictly limited to the variables chosen. In all cases, however, the analogy with real life falls short as the players, especially in the inter-nation type of simulations, are frequently torn between the conflicting demands of simulating what they regard as real nation behaviour and of optimizing the game outcomes through behaviour most suited to it, e.g. cheating. Moreover, although they generally enthusiastically fall into their roles, they only play a game whereas in real life the decision-makers face decisions of real, sometimes life and death consequences.

The simulation techniques are widely employed as a teaching device. Undoubtedly the technique is attractive by stimulating the participants both to acquire information about the situation and to apply it in a dynamic way. It is impossible to measure the effectiveness of the learning process but, in all likelihood, what occurs under the stress of gaming is not so much the process of learning as it is a reinforced and heightened awareness of things previously known. For theory-building, simulation has been useful by forcing its authors to develop variables operational within the simulation play. This enables them to find out relationships which may not occur to us in the study of the more complex real world and thus sharpen our appreciation of the latter. This is, for instance, true about the complex interaction between domestic constraints and foreign policy.

In policy-making, all the three types have been sponsored and the first two also widely employed by United States governmental agencies—the Political–Military Exercise for specific situations, in order to clarify tactics and short-term strategies, the Inter-Nation Simulation to explore more general policies. TEMPER results have remained academic. The raising of a host of theoretical questions involved in the construction and the analysis of simulation has been beneficial to the theoreticians involved but the information and the predictions are too abstract to be useful not only in day-to-day but also in long-range policy-making.

Prediction. Forecasting falls into two distinct categories—point and pattern prediction. The former is of direct use for governmental action, to assist in choosing among the perceived options at short range; the latter is concerned with the longer range and with sequences or groups of events. Exact prediction of individual events depends upon two presuppositions: first, that there are involved calculable, i.e. quantitatively expressible factors, and, second, that the essential factors can be really known and accurately measured. These presuppositions obviously do not obtain with regard to human behaviour concerning which, as in meteorology, forecasts cannot be certain but are merely probability judgements of various degrees. The practical results are similarly limited, too, and prediction is not a precise guide to action, whether we have to decide about taking an umbrella or about preparing for the possibilities of war.

Prediction of probable future states is, of course, the basis of our expectations and hence a major source of behaviour. Perhaps the closest analogy lies with economics where expectations play a central role in some analyses and in all planning. Expectations are the core of what are often called 'naïve models' used for the analysis of businessmen's forecasts and as actual forecasting devices. These models are based upon the notion that the future is simply a function of the past. One type assumes complete identity; another, more sophisticated one, assumes that the change from the present will equal that in the period just preceding the present, i.e. the existing trends will continue; the third one assumes that the future will be the weighted average of past periods. There is some evidence that actual business decisions are made on these lines. All the predictions based upon such simple models are obviously highly uncertain but the refinement of models as a device for prediction beyond the first few steps has not notably improved performance.[19] Moreover, even a high statistical probability does not ensure that an individual decision will necessarily prove right.

The failure of economic theory to provide a reliable basis for prediction raises doubts about the feasibility of reliable predictions in the much more complex political field. Moreover, the limited number of States offers more limited opportunities for the calculation of statistical probabilities than is available in much consumer research. This, of course, does not mean that some mathematical models of equal *theoretical* power may not be devised. The accomplished mathematical theory of war developed by Lewis F. Richardson is a good example. In the analysis of A. Rapoport the logical advantages of such a theory are as follows: 'Whereas adherents of verbal theories may engage in desultory arguments about whether shows of strength are conducive to peace or war the builder of a mathematical theory can combine both assumptions (seemingly contradictory when stated in ordinary language) and reduce the question to one about the relative effects of the one and the other tendency.'[20]

The approaching end of our millennium has served as a tempting terminal date for recent attempts at futurology, i.e. the forecasting of future scenarios. The ambitious 1967 book by Herman Kahn and Anthony J. Wiener, *The Year 2000* bases forecasts of the likely future of the international system on a combination of the analysis of economic and demographic trends (which of course can drastically change) and of speculation about strategic and political stability and instability which is ingenious but idiosyncratic. The Commission on the Year 2000 established by the American Academy of Arts and Sciences has set up a working group on the future of the international system but it remains to be seen how far this group will manage to go beyond Kahn and Wiener's sweeping generalizations.

Europe's Futures, Europe's Choices: Models of Western Europe in the 1970s edited by A. Buchan, is much more modest both in its basis and in its time span. It consists mainly of a logical analysis of a range of possible alternative political structures for Western Europe. The study offers a convenient though scarcely 'scientific' approach to mid-term planning based upon the choice between the alternatives which, rather impressionistically, seem most plausible.

However imprecise, prediction has a bearing upon actual policy. This is clearly so in economics as 'the decision-makers' (producers, governors, and even consumers) are, to a fair extent, familiar with the economic forecasts so that these, in a self-fulfilling fashion, exercise a direct, although by no means decisive, influence upon their behaviour. If futurology is to make further progress in the analysis of international futures, its influence may come closer to that of economic prediction. The importance of prediction would thus be found not in a precise forecasting of trends, which is impossible, but in increasing our awareness of these trends and thus enabling us to determine with greater precision the range of possibilities and the parameters of action. We will, also, be better equipped to adjust more rapidly and rationally to sudden change; the use of comparisons serves a similar purpose.

Prediction plays an important part in the normatively oriented approaches to international theory. Instead of postulating automatic responses, policy oriented predictions can aim at fashioning governmental responses in the desired direction—be it positively, as the integrationists do in favour of a Western European union, or negatively, as the adherents of peace research and conflict resolution schools do trying to prevent violent conflict and war.

3
Systems Analysis and Allied Approaches

1. THE NATURE OF SYSTEMS ANALYSIS

SYSTEMS analysis is used mainly in application to the international global system and therefore it is less useful for the direct analysis of foreign policy than are other approaches. Its main use is to enable us to see foreign policy in the broadest possible context, to discern within it patterns and to compare these patterns with those appearing in the foreign policies of other states.

Systems analysis is discussed here first because it is fundamental and because it expresses in the clearest and most general fashion the basic objective of all theory—to think systematically about the field of inquiry; moreover, all other theories can be easily and naturally related to systems analysis. A certain degree of confusion can arise from the similarity of the words 'systematic' and 'systemic'. In a way, anybody who has systematically reflected about the nature of international reality will find much that is familiar to him in the systems analysis approach and may even discover that he has been employing it without labelling it with a distinctive name, like Molière's Mr. Jourdain when he discovered that all his life he had been employing prose. There is, however, as will be pointed out, more to systems analysis than a mere elaboration, often in difficult vocabulary, of certain common-sense notions; its stress upon the inter-connectedness of all factors and events is important as a general orientation.

The concept 'system' in International Relations is a direct derivation of this concept as used in General Systems Theory (GST) which constitutes an effort to find a basic correlation be-

tween all areas of knowledge. Because of this fundamental objective, studies in this field tend to be multi-disciplinary and hence
attractive as a potential source of many insights and inspirations
for the theoreticians of International Relations, who came late to
the systems field.

The concept 'system' has been very widely but also very con-
fusedly employed in social sciences.[1] The definition can centre
upon a group of actors interacting within the system's structure by
recognizable processes and subject to various constraints, or on the
various processes of interaction. The many definitions do not
deviate from the general systems theory which defines 'systems' as
anything formed of parts placed together or adjusted into a regu-
lar and connected whole; an assemblage of bodies as a connected
whole.

The copious literature on the subject discusses either 'ideal
type' systems based on their differentiation by essential characteristics, or actual historical international systems, as can be dis-
cerned in the past and present, or some combination of both. It
refers mainly to the widest, at present global system, but some of it
analyses subordinate systems such as regions or individual States
conceived as political systems.

The advantage of employing the term 'international system'
instead of the traditional 'family of nations', 'international society', or 'world community' is found in the fact that it attempts to
employ 'scientific' thinking and to distinguish clear variables and
patterns—whereas the older concepts have been used loosely and
interchangeably without such purpose. Moreover, we are already
used to thinking about social affairs in terms of 'systems'—about
personality systems, economic and social systems, and often also
about world affairs, e.g. when using the frequent phrases about
stability or tensions growing or lessening.

The systemic approach is valuable in enabling us to analyse
the behaviour of States within its proper setting or settings and,
instead of unduly concentrating upon one State, to pay due regard
to its interaction with the external environment; in any analysis of
foreign policy, systemic variables are essential as part of the explanation and their systematic study is bound to pay off. Indeed,
in the 'micro-studies' of the individual States, we are overwhelmed
with unique occurrences and situations which, of course, are valuable for their own sake as historical evidence, but we find it diffi-

cult to isolate any regularities and patterns in political behaviour which would enable us to compare and generalize.

If we conceive of international phenomena as a system, this introduces a basic source of regularities. The main variables distinguished in all international systems can be meaningfully clustered in three large groups: first, the actions of States as components of the system; second, the structure and functioning of the system which results from the interaction of its units; third, the environmental factors which condition both the actions of the units and the operation of the system.

2. CONCEPTUAL ISSUES AND POSTULATES

In the analysis of Oran Young, which is here closely followed, some basic conceptual issues arise in all systemic approaches:

(*a*) Although in practice the two approaches do not fundamentally differ, the empirical identification of a system can be based either upon the conception of the existence of natural systems the criteria of which can be specified, or upon a constructivist notion that, for the purpose of analysis, any collection of data can be treated as a system. From either approach, the identification of individual systems and their boundaries gives rise to disputes, e.g. the various scholars cannot agree when precisely the international system has become global or whether we are now entering a new, multipolar system and, if so, what was the starting point of the process of the transformation of the bipolar system into it.

(*b*) There is general agreement on the essential variables being the units (or actors), structures, processes, and context.

(*c*) The global system is divided into subsystems—either on geographical lines into regional groupings, or on functional lines.

(*d*) Concrete constructs focus on the physical components of phenomena whereas analytic constructs concentrate upon selected aspects of these phenomena. The former do not require many assumptions but are unsuitable for broad generalizations; the latter run the risk of becoming completely divorced from reality.

(*e*) When we are concerned with the global political international system, economic, social, technological, and cultural factors are best encompassed under the term 'context'. If we deal not with the global but with a regional system, the other regional subsystems and the global system can be conceived as the 'environment'.

(*f*) The theoreticians are generally well aware of the dangers of 'organismic analogies', and such commonplace statements as about the State or its Government acting, are clearly understood as a shorthand expression of complex processes and not as a description of reality.

3. THE INDEPENDENT VARIABLES

All systems analysts distinguish units (or actors), structures, processes, and context (or environment) as major elements in every system. These elements can be considered as major factors in the terms of which all substantive phenomena are explained, or 'independent' variables. They are:

(*a*) A unit or actor in the international system is a formally organized entity (which in itself can be subjected to systems analysis) that is (at least indirectly) composed of human beings and is not wholly subordinate to any other actors in effective terms. The States, in our century the nation-states, constitute the most outstanding type of actors in the contemporary international systems; for a while this led to the tendency to restrict analysis to them. There is a certain ambiguity even in this category when we deal with units dominated by other States (The People's Republic of Mongolia) or with breakaway units during periods of struggle (Biafra). International organizations are another important class; here the ambiguity of their position is often even greater as clearly seen in the confused growth of the diplomacy conducted by the E.E.C. directly as an organization. Political and trade union associations, religious bodies, and international consortia form other groups of actors in which it is frequently hard to determine with certainty the degree of their dependence upon individual States and therefore their qualification as actors.

Apart from the definition of actors other than States, a fruitful field of analysis lies in attempts at classifying States according to some important characteristics and generalizing about the groups. The contemporary classification based upon power into Super-Powers, Middle Powers, and Small Powers is of obvious interest to Britain when she is seeking analogies and comparisons with the behaviour of other 'Middle Powers'; distinction between developed and developing States, or between status quo and revisionist States, serve as convenient bases of analysis.

(*b*) The term 'structures' refers to the characteristic relationships among the actors across time. Various types of association, from formal alliances to informal groupings, come under consideration as well as types of hostile interaction, giving rise to the familiar distinction between bipolar and multipolar systems, blocs, etc. International system structures tend to be informal rather than formal and pose many so far not fully explored problems for analysis such as that of status, of 'social distance', etc.

(*c*) Processes can be distinguished from structures both through analytic properties and through time scale—they refer to forms and modes of interaction instead of characteristic relationships, and they encompass individual interactions whereas structures deal only with regularities across time. There are several major ways of analysing processes—through their instruments (military, diplomatic, economic, etc.), their mode (bilateral, multilateral) and degree of formality, according to their place in the spectrum between conflict and co-operation or coercion and persuasion, etc. The physical factors prescribing the parameters of action are introduced as 'constraints' whereas other factors affecting the process are often analysed as 'rules of the game'.

(*d*) The context of the international political system is usually divided into science and technology, economics, physical, social, and cultural dimensions.

All the time attempts are being made to analyse in some orderly way the organized complexity as a whole or at least a substantial part of it. As all the elements are closely interconnected, formal, mathematical procedures in the systemic analysis of politics are here of limited use. In order to manipulate the variables (often on the 'if ... then' pattern of economics) we have to reduce them to manageable numbers; this involves us in making assumptions which take us too far away from real life.

4. THE DEPENDENT VARIABLES

The systems approach can be used to explain any international phenomena which are, for the purposes of analysis, treated as 'dependent variables'. Most analyses cluster around the following somewhat overlapping five major categories, with a great degree of variety within them:

(*a*) 'Power', which is a fundamental political phenomenon, is variously defined, but all definitions refer to the capacity of making others behave as we wish them to do. It is so central and all-pervading that some thinkers refer to it as 'political money' and many have been tempted to focus their analysis around it. Unfortunately the concept of 'power' defies rigorous analysis. Three distinct images of the concept are current: first, as a possession, or piece of property; second, as a moving force resembling the flow of energy on an electric circuit; third, as an attribute of traits in human relations. In many writings the boundaries between these three images are blurred.

Attempts have been made to define the major dimensions of power (e.g. domain, scope, weight, and coerciveness).[2] Major distinctions are made between the various elements of power; 'power potential' and 'actual power' as exercised in specific situations, 'putative power' which, in the opinion of others, the actor could exercise in various situations if he were to make an effort (determining the power status). Distinctions between actual and putative power helped to analyse the position of Britain at the outbreak of the Boer War or to compare the postwar evolution of the foreign policies of Britain, on the one hand, and of Germany and Japan on the other. Much attention has been devoted to the analysis of various instruments of power, of their applicability to conflict and to co-operation and their usefulness in various types of international systems (e.g. now within the nuclear context) and within different sets of relationships. Specific hypotheses about particular forms of power within individual international systems have been advanced and, hopefully, we may reach the position in which we may be able to undertake a limited amount of prediction.

(*b*) 'Management of power' is a concept referring to the central problem of the regulation of power which is often used to describe and classify international systems. Thus we can find direct control under imperial and colonial systems, indirect control with fairly articulated spheres of influence in hegemonial types, a condominium pattern when the leading actors co-operate in controlling major functional issues on a system wide basis (e.g. the Concert of Europe in relation to the smaller States). Power can be managed by balancing it in the various types of balance of power or through community arrangements that do not involve straightforward power relationships (cf. the shift in the postwar French attitudes to the management of the power of Germany). Tentative hypotheses have been advanced about the crucial aspects of the varying patterns of power management, especially relating to their origin, stability, political and economic implications, and mutual interrelationships between the varying patterns; some of these may be directly relevant for the analysis of the problems facing Britain in the future organization of Western European security.

(c) 'Stability' is a frequently explored aspect of international systems. It is sometimes confusingly applied either to 'structural stability', i.e. the continuation across time of the essential variables of the system without major change, or to 'dynamic stability' which denotes a tendency to move towards an equilibrium following disturbances. The opposite term of 'instability' should be distinguished in its latent or potential and its actual forms. To relate 'stability' to the other concepts, there is a link between stability and management of power as stability postulates at least minimally effective arrangements for the management of power although it does not correlate in all respects with the other problem. Change (discussed below[3]) can disrupt stability, whether statically or dynamically conceived, but not necessarily so; indeed, change can actually increase stability by reducing the elements of instability without producing qualitative changes in the essential variables of the system.

Turning to the question of the stability of the present system, various authors point out that we lack the homogeneity of States sometimes postulated as a precondition (Kant postulated republics, Metternich monarchies), and that we are ideologically divided; in the presence of only two Super-Powers, the operation of an effective balance of power system of the nineteenth-century pattern is impossible; in the technological context within which no actor, not even the Super-Powers, can regard themselves as secure ('unconditionally viable'), the system is bound to be actively unstable. Others, however, contend that all these, although important sources of latent instability, do not necessarily lead to active instability; indeed, some go to the length of asserting that the new technological context and the emerging 'rules of the game' ensure a greater stability of the international system, which involves a much greater chance of the survival of its recognized units, even these extremely weak ('not viable'), than in its nineteenth-century predecessor.

(*d*) 'Change' in international systems is a complex phenomenon which generally occurs in interrelated patterns both in the independent and in the dependent variables identified above. Theoreticians have been widely concerned with identifying the analytically important dimensions of 'change'—its extensiveness or scope, its smooth or abrupt fashion, the degree to which it is patterned, its 'spill-over' effect, its pace, the nature and degree of interdependence between the factors conducive to it, its 'directionality' (which distinguishes between cumulative and non-cumulative types). Many hypotheses have been advanced about the various relevant factors, e.g. in a bipolar system changes are likely to be more extensive, abrupt and independent whereas in a multipolar system they are likely to be more evolutionary, interdependent, and cumulative.

(*e*) 'System-transformation' refers to a qualitative change in one or more essential variables. Here a distinction must be made between a 'breakdown' and a 'transition' to another system. Some of the leading hypotheses deal with the degree of interdependence between the units as a factor increasing the likelihood of system transformation or the role of a dominant or 'core actor' in the evolution of an extensive community where community links are only slightly developed.

There is, of course, no inherent logic in choosing some factors and phenomena as being the explanation of others (independent variables) and other factors and phenomena as being explained through them (dependent variables). It all depends upon our interests and convenience. As any rigid scheme can readily become very remote from real life, some theoreticians introduce intervening variable factors which they deem relevant but which they do not wish to classify fully either among the causes or among the effects. For example, instead of analysing the effect of bipolarity and multipolarity upon the stability of the international system, we can introduce the factor of nuclear technology and ask whether it is not decisive in dividing the systems into dichotomous classes. It seems plausible that bipolar systems prove stable and multipolar systems less stable when nuclear technology exists although the reverse seems to have been the case in the non-nuclear past.

5. GENERAL EVALUATION

The greatest advantage of the systems approach lies in its comprehensive nature. Whichever the focus of our interest, whichever the technique most suitable for our analysis, we can correlate it with our favourite variant of the systems theory. The theory is limited in its explanatory power but is generally useful in its broad capacity to enable us to organize the disjointed elements and in formulating interesting hypotheses. It is most frequently applied to the global system but it is also helpful in analysing the place of regions and of single States within it. Thus we distinguish three levels of analysis: first the dominant, global system; second, subordinate (regional) systems; and third, internal systems (of States). Within a subordinate (regional) system we can distinguish a core sector, a peripheral sector, and an intrusive system.

Like most behavioural schools of theory, the systems approach suffers from a number of shortcomings:

(*a*) The theoreticians have been unable to agree upon and define satisfactorily the numbers and types of actors, the main variables, and the parameters of action. Most of the major books on the subject endeavour to establish the author's own methodology and classifications so that combination and comparison of the insights is often difficult. Some progress towards standardization of concepts and unification of methods, has, however, been made in the last few years.

(*b*) Generally, the treatment of international systems does not allow sufficient relevance to the volitional and normative aspects of State behaviour and of system interrelationships.

(*c*) Carrying a 'macro', i.e. global system bias, it is not directly helpful in explaining foreign policy problems.

(*d*) The various treatments accord an important role to the analysis of change but the concept of 'change' has so far proved too complex to allow of a convincing analysis.

6. THE LINKAGE APPROACH

This is one of the latest theoretical approaches.[4] It has not yet been fully elaborated, but like systems analysis, it offers a common ground for many variants and has proved attractive to many scholars. Its starting point is systems analysis, as 'linkage' denotes any recurrent sequence of behaviour that originates in one system and is reacted to in another. It thus offers more systematic tools of analysis for the investigation of the perennial problems of the nexus between domestic politics and foreign policy by regarding the domestic and the international political spheres as two systems in interaction. The initial and the terminal stages of linkage are described as 'inputs' and 'outputs' and are differentiated according to their origin within the State or within its external environment. If the patterns of behaviour are deliberately designed, the inputs and outputs are 'direct'; if these patterns are unanticipated, the inputs and outputs are 'indirect'.

Inputs and outputs are linked together by three major types of linkages: the penetrative, the reactive, and the emulative. A 'penetrative' linkage is defined as one in which one polity serves as a participant in the political processes of another and shares the authority to allocate values within the penetrated unit. The category embraces not only political and military but also economic penetration and could be usefully employed in the analysis of the domination of industries and economies by massive foreign investment. Quite different is a 'reactive' linkage which is caused by boundary-crossing reactions without direct foreign participation in the decisions made within the unit. Those responsible for the input do not penetrate the other unit but, nevertheless, those responsible for the outputs with the unit do react; e.g. in a relationship of perceived hostility, an increase in the offensive capacity on one side clearly leads to an increase in the defence effort on the other. A special variety linkage is the 'emulative' one where the response takes essentially the same form as the action triggering it off. One can distinguish here a diffusion or demonstration effect whereby political activities in one country are perceived and emulated in another. The concept can be applied to all states which have followed the United States in developing nuclear weapons, to the spread of social welfare measures in the West, claims for liberalization of the political systems and for greater national independence in the East of Europe, claims for independence by colonial units, etc. Rosenau's concept can do with an additional refinement by dividing this linkage into 'emulative' where the polity reaching can expect to match the initiating State whereas in cases where the action is imitated without any expectations of matching, the process becomes 'imitative'. Thus the French decision to develop nuclear weapons would be classed as clearly imitative in relation to the Super-Powers but emulative in relation to Britain.

The 'linkage' approach is useful because it neither denies nor exaggerates the relevance of national boundaries, saving its users from the distortions arising from more extreme views about their relevance. Most theoreticians are now well aware of the limitations of studying the State units as if they were isolated. Some of them, however, tend to succumb to the other extreme of contending that interdependence within the international system (e.g. in social communications) has reached such proportions that it has become useless to recognize the boundaries and to distinguish between what is going on within them and outside them: obviously they cannot generate any insights into the different impacts of the various national systems or on the sources, location, or relative potency of the international phenomena.

The linkage scheme relates to recurrent patterns of behaviour and not to isolated phenomena and Rosenau has offered a general framework for analysis by a matrix (see Diagram II) combining different features of the polity on the one hand and different types of the external environments on the other. One axis identifies different types of actors, attitudes, institutions, and processes which are central features of the polity for this type of analysis; the other axis distinguishes the contiguous, regional, Cold War, racial, resource, and organizational environments. This yields 144 areas in which national–international linkages can be formed.

This complex and elaborate scheme is clearly vulnerable to severe criticisms, e.g. the distinction between the various environments leaves much to be desired. Moreover, it is extremely difficult to apply it to real life. The eleven case-studies included in Rosenau's volume do not, with one exception, fully apply the scheme and the same can be said of many of the papers subsequently submitted to the Fifteenth International Political Science Congress for the session devoted to this approach. And yet

DIAGRAM II. A proposed linkage framework.

Polity	Environmental → Outputs and Inputs	The Contiguous Environment	The Regional Environment	The Cold War Environment	The Racial Environment	The Resource Environment	The Organizational Environment
Actors	1. Executive Officials						
	2. Legislative Officials						
	3. Civilian Bureaucrats						
	4. Military Bureaucrats						
	5. Political Parties						
	6. Interest Groups						
	7. Elite Groups						
Attitudes	8. Ideology						
	9. Political Culture						
	10. Public Opinion						
Institutions	11. Executive						
	12. Legislatures						
	13. Bureaucracies						
	14. Military Establishments						
	15. Elections						
	16. Party Systems						
	17. Communications Systems						
	18. Social Institutions						
Processes	19. Socialization and Recruitment						
	20. Interest Articulation						
	21. Interest Aggregation						
	22. Policy-Making						
	23. Policy-Administration						
	24. Integrative-Disintegrative						

the approach has generated really interesting investigations which probably would not have occurred without it, especially essays comparing the element of 'insularity' as a common factor in the foreign policies of Britain, Japan, and Ceylon, and the element of non-conformity in alliance in the foreign policies of China and France.

7. ADAPTIVE BEHAVIOUR

An interesting offspring of the linkage approach concerned with the elusive nature of change has been proposed by its own author through applying to the behaviour of States the basic scheme outlined in W. Ross Ashby's *Design for a Brain*, and through analysing 'Foreign Policy as Adaptive Behaviour'.[5] In Rosenau's words:

... the basic premise of the adaptive perspective [is] that all nations can be viewed as adapting entities with similar problems that arise out of the need to cope with their environment. The adaptive perspective seeks understanding not in unique factors, but in common factors; not through the case study, but through the comparative assessment; not through the applied inquiry that solves immediate problems, but through the theoretical formulation that tests hypotheses and establishes general principles. (p. 366)

The definition of the key concept is simple and its elements are not rigidly determined but are left to empirical definition. 'Any foreign policy behaviour undertaken by the government is conceived to be adaptive when it copes with or stimulates changes in the external environment that contributes to keeping the essential structures of the society within acceptable limits.' The opposite, maladaptive behaviour, contributes to changes in essential structures that are outside acceptable limits. Coping with the constant flow of trans-boundary transactions, a government embarks sometimes on adaptive and sometimes on maladaptive policies; the relationship between the two, as well as the relative importance of the issues dealt with, determines the position of the State in terms of adaptation. Extremes are very rare—cases of complete maladaptation can be found in States losing a war and forfeiting independence; complete adaptation would mean the maintenance of essential structures fully static. With the growing rate and speed of change, the adaptive capacities of society are increasingly called into action and greater fluctuations between the extremes of adaptation and maladaptation can be expected.

Adaptation invariably involves change and this can be classified according to its degree both within the domestic and the external sectors as change in personnel, political change, and socio-economic change. This classification facilitates hypotheses about the nature and scope of the adaptations likely to be sought; for example, it seems clear that major rapid socio-economic changes at home demand corresponding socio-economic adaptations in the salient external environment (cf. the case of Castro's Cuba) and, likewise, that major changes in the political and socio-economic external environment require major adaptation in these fields at home (cf. the case of Britain and the growth of Western European Communities). Finally, the modes of change can be classified according to whether they rank high or low on the domestic or the external axis.

Again, the scheme amounts to a restatement of what must seem fairly obvious to anybody who has been active in the field of foreign policy whether as a practitioner or as a theoretician. As Rosenau himself admits, the value of the approach for empirical studies is at the moment dubious, as there seems to be no clear way of defining what is 'essential' or 'acceptable'—the notions are unclear even at any given point of time and are, moreover, constantly changing (cf. the great shift between the three applications in the British definition of what is acceptable to her in the rules of the E.E.C.). Moreover this adaptive behaviour refers clearly to past and present changes but involves also an element of forecasting based upon some 'strategic images' of the environment[6] which are never clearly determined. Finally, there seem to be no criteria for the evaluation of any move within the adaptive-maladaptive scale even *ex-post*, in terms of its outcome; e.g. if the physical stability of the Western European States has remained intact after more than twenty years of NATO's existence, this provides no clear clue for the question whether the 'adaptive behaviour' designed to maintain NATO has contributed to this stability as we cannot be sure whether the postulated threat of a Soviet attack would have materialized in the absence of NATO.

Nevertheless, although it is impossible to analyse the 'what-may-have-beens', focusing on 'adapting behaviour' enables us to look systematically at what happens between the sources and the consequences of foreign policy. This is particularly important in a period when rapid adaptation is essential in the most important areas of life. Baffling questions of what is acceptable in economic or strategic dependence upon another State or in limiting sovereignty in favour of international organization may be more clearly analysed in terms of adaptation as well as transformation of the national system.

4
Integration Theory and the Functionalist Thesis

1. THEIR CENTRAL PLACE IN CONTEMPORARY INTERNATIONAL THEORY

SYSTEMS analysis relates to the fundamental modes of thinking about the international system and does not readily lend itself to empirical work; the approaches centring upon States, which are discussed in the next two chapters, are closer to political reality but defy attempts at general theory. Integration theory and functionalism occupy an in-between position, combining several theories of integration with a great and rapidly growing volume of empirical investigation.

Apart from the United States, no area of the world has been subjected to as minute political analysis as the six members of the European Community; the E.E.C is a living laboratory for the integration theory. Again with the possible exception of the United States, the links between theory and political life are nowhere as close. Theories of integration, especially those of Ernst Haas, have undoubtedly been influential in the development of the Communities; the evolving processes within the Communities have been continuously subjected to theoretical analysis which has, in turn, led to the evolution and, to a fair extent, also to the revision of theory. Although, as may well be expected, the theoreticians do not agree among themselves and produce divergent predictions, they supply at least a fairly solid analytical foundation for thinking about the future. Finally, and not unimportantly, in the unprecedented and confused political situation in Western Europe, the analysis and predictions can have a considerable impact upon the actual future outcomes by shaping the expectations of the major actors and by providing argumentation for and against certain policies. Focusing mainly on Western Europe but, in later years, dealing increasingly also with other regions, the writers have brought to bear upon the subject a great variety of techniques and approaches, especially systems analysis, cybernetical study of learning processes, and theories of decision-making and bargaining. They have, also, amassed a great quantity of relevant social, economic, and political data.

Integration theory has thus become an umbrella for a great variety of approaches but it contains an important core of original theory which, moreover, being uniquely tied to real life, has been rapidly evolving with the growth and the evolution of regional communities. Functionalism, in its contemporary, neo-functionalist form, is now no more than one of the few leading theories of integration. In its original form, however, functionalism preceded the integration theory and hence will be discussed first. As, to some extent like peace research, it has a strongly normative flavour, it will be distinctively referred to as the 'functionalist thesis' rather than approach.

2. THE FUNCTIONALIST THESIS[1]

The starting point of functionalism is that the dominant organizational unit of the international system, the nation-state, is becoming increasingly inadequate for satisfying the needs of mankind because it is confined to circumscribed territory, whereas the needs of man cut across its boundaries. To quote the school's prominent critical exponent, Inis Claude (p. 348):

The state system imposes an arbitrary and rigid system of vertical division upon global society, disrupting the global unity of the whole, and carving the world into segments whose separateness is jealously guarded by sovereignties which are neither able to solve the fundamental problems nor willing to permit them to be solved by other authorities.

Functionalism constitutes more than a theory; it is, in fact a philosophy based upon attempts to eliminate frictions inherent in interstate relations, including war, either by concentrating upon the economic and social welfare of the people of the world, and ignoring State boundaries, or by setting up international organizations devoted to the various activities and functions arising from the satisfaction of man's socio-economic needs.

In the original formulation by Mitrany which reflects the Marxist stress upon the primacy of economics (to which social needs are added), politics would yield to the socio-economic basis, and, once international society is organized in a functionalist way with a network of organizations catering for its multifarious needs, the tendency to and eventually the very possibility of war would be overcome and man would be on the road to everlasting peace. The early functionalists assumed that war is not based upon aggressive propensities inherent in human nature but upon the way this nature is conditioned by the present system; new institutions, traditions and ideas bring about new, more peaceful patterns of behaviour. In a retrospective evaluation, the functional thesis about wars became more moderate: '... the experience of successful co-operation in the wide range of welfare areas now amenable to international administration in modern industrial States would gradually reduce the possibilities of violence about national objectives and would strengthen an ethos of co-operation.'[2]

Another functionalist assumption is that the process would be cumulative and that functional development in one field would foster and engender similar types of co-operation in other fields and, moreover, that this 'spill-over' effect would not be limited in scope but that 'the learning process' would eventually affect the very core of the present international system, i.e. the institution of the sovereign State. As the organizations would start in relatively unimportant non-controversial socio-economic fields, the existence of a few such organizations clearly would not transform international society but a large number of them would become politically decisive.

The divisive subjective allegiances to individual States which lead to wars would be gradually replaced by new loyalties fostered by the new, cross-national units which would counteract harmful nationalist attitudes. The functionalists believe that, as these new organizations proceed to show their value to humanity by meeting all the needs that States find unmanageable, including the overwhelming problems of underdevelopment, poverty, and inequality, people would willingly transfer their allegiance and a new 'functional' international society would arise in which the major units would be based upon *function* rather than *territory*. In Mitrany's words, functionalism would thus 'overlay political divisions with a spreading web of international relations and agencies in which and through which the interests and life of all nations would be gradually integrated.'

The functionalist creed is clearly vulnerable to many criticisms, the most fundamental of which concern its assumption that the ties of individuals with their nation-states are basically rational. Claude cogently points out several other weaknesses: the dubious validity of the assumption that underdevelopment, poverty, and inequality cause war; about the 'spillover' effect from one sector into another; about the possibility of separating socio-economic from political questions; about the likelihood of the evolution of functional integration in the face of the probable political crises; about the ability of individuals to transfer their loyalties from a State to an international organization.

This is not so much a refutation of theory as a challenge to a *Weltanschauung*; neither the functionalists nor their critics can supply empirical evidence clearly supporting their respective views. Some interesting and fairly readily testable hypotheses tangentially arising from the debate relate to the peculiarly exposed position of the international civil servants:

(1) International institutions undermine national loyalties in their officials and replace them with loyalty to themselves. This hypothesis has been clearly governing the attitudes of Communist States on their representatives in such institutions—they rotate them frequently and, at first, were reluctant to appoint more than nominal numbers. On the other hand, psychological theory, supported by some actual investigations conducted by Professor Guetzkov, discovered no fundamental clash; on the contrary, individuals seem to have a propensity towards and develop a habit of loyalty, and the best international civil servants are recruited among individuals loyal to their own countries rather than convinced 'internationalists' who are rootless and lack the habit of loyalty.

Closely allied are less far-reaching hypotheses:

(2) that because the international officials conceive their respective

national interests differently from State officials, they tend to promote international unity;

(3) that non-govenmental bodies give support to international officials in this respect; and

(4) that consensus among experts upon some functional problems leads to consensus among the politicians whereas the lack of such expert consensus leads to a corresponding lack of political consensus.

Functionalism was not limited to pure theorizing or to normative rules. It was based upon and reinforced by the rapid growth of international organizations from the mid-nineteenth century: in the fields of communications (post and telecommunications), international rivers (the Rhine and the Danube), some scientific enterprises (the Geodetic Union). The successful evolution of these international 'bureaux' greatly influenced Jan Smuts, leading to the distinctly functionalist provisions of articles 23–5 of the League of Nations Covenant. The International Labour Organization was established and the functionalist work of the League, especially of Nansen on behalf of refugees or of Rajchman in the domain of world health, were so successful that, after the political débâcle of the League, serious proposals were made to reform the League to become a largely functionalist body. Further functional agencies were established during World War II and the organizations were loosely tied with the United Nations as 'Specialized Agencies'. Also non-governmental international organizations have rapidly proliferated. According to the not particularly reliable *Yearbook of the Union of International Associations*, the figures have been growing as follows:

Category	1956/7	1966/7	1968/9
Governmental			
U.N. family	17	25	28
European Communities	1	9	10
Other Inter-Governmental Organizations	114	165	191
Total	132	199	229
Total Non-Governmental Organizations	985	1,935	2,188
Total International Organizations	1,117	2,134	2,417

Obviously there is a great variety of social needs which cannot be fully satisfied on a limited national scale and call for a boundary-crossing organization. When a need is felt, whether it be concerned with the basic problems of pollution or peripheral hobbies like philately, an appropriate institution is eventually established. The momentum of international organization is such that it is possible today to pose the hypothesis that the process is becoming circular and that, once established, organizations create their own functions and, as they grow, new functions develop from them.

The most fundamental question with which the functionalists are concerned is that whether economic and social integration inevitably lead to political union. Here the functionalist approach merges into the theory of integration which is discussed in the following section.[3]

3. THE EVOLUTION OF INTEGRATION THEORY

Integration theory, much of which has centred upon the evolution of the Communities in Western Europe, is of obvious interest to Britain now that it is poised to enter these Communities. The question which divides the theoreticians, whether a political union would inevitably follow economic unification, could become the centre of the domestic political debate on entry rather than the details about which we have negotiated. Unfortunately, the theoreticians fundamentally disagree, although, in their arguments, they shed some light upon the relevant problems.

To start with, the integration theory is connected with the broad analysis of social communication, started by Professor K. W. Deutsch. In his pioneering work on *Political Community at the International Level*, published in 1954, Professor Deutsch inaugurated a prolific school concerned with 'international transactions'. He argued in his book that international community can be ascertained and measured through the volume, content, and scope of international transactions between its hypothesized members. Subsequent emperical work at Princeton which resulted in *Political Community and the North Atlantic Area* (1957) validated Deutsch's thesis. Some rather naïve hypotheses originally advanced about the inevitability of integration in the presence of an increased flow of international transactions were soon abandoned. Deutsch himself became pessimistic, claiming that with the growth of social communications *intra*-national transactions grow at a more rapid rate than *inter*-national transactions, leading away rather than towards international integration. In the balanced analysis of Donald J. Puchala,[4] we are not exactly clear, either theoretically or empirically, about the processes of change in transactions. Analysis of these changes, the methodology of which is rapidly advancing, helps us to *describe* regional integration but not to *explain* it; transaction flows *do not cause* integration.

The process of State unification is, of course, not a new subject and the literature devoted to the formation of unions or federations as well as the analysis of 'supranational' organizations all refer to phenomena closely related to 'integration'. The latter concept remains poorly defined.[5] There is general agreement that 'integration' refers to co-operative but not to coercive unification efforts. The main semantic confusion arises around the use of the term to describe either the *process* or the *outcome*. It is possible to think of '... the process whereby nations forego the desire and ability to conduct foreign and key domestic politics independently of each other, seeking instead to make *joint decisions* or *to delegate* the decision-making process to new control organs', or 'the evolution over time of a collective decision-making system among nations.[6] On the other hand, in order to distinguish the concept of 'regional integration' from the overlapping concepts of 'regionalism', 'regional co-operation', 'regional organization', 'regional movements', 'regional systems', etc., it seems more precise to restrict the term 'integration' to the terminal condition. This is the meaning in which Amitai Etzioni, one of the earliest theoreticians of integration, has always proposed and to which Ernst Haas has now become converted.

Most of the analysis has been devoted to regional integration attempts, first mainly in Western Europe, lately also in other regions. The most advanced theoretician in the field is Ernst Haas who has also been extremely influential in his contribution to the evolution of the E.E.C. through his influence upon the thinking of its officials and of the members of the Commission. Haas may be termed a 'neo-functionalist'. The neo-functionalist method shifts from the broadly philosophical one of the original functionalists to the more 'scientific' one now in fashion. Moreover, instead of somewhat unrealistically centring upon consensus, it regards competition among different interests as more fundamental; here the theory links up with the modern conflict theory.[7] It claims that, as consensus is unattainable, stability can be secured only through efficient management of conflict within a pluralist society. The neo-functionalists generally agree that economic integration will lead to political union. In the words of Ernst Haas: 'Under modern conditions the relationship between economic and political union had best be treated as a continuum.' Those disagreeing with such conclusions, like Stanley Hoffmann, stand somewhat outside the mainstream of neo-functionalism.

The dynamics of the process are assumed to work in favour of political integration despite disintegrative incidents and tendencies. The initial steps towards integration are economic but this has important political implications in decisions as to how much national autonomy, i.e. sovereignty, it is necessary to delegate to the new union. Although crises occur over the need to take political decisions, disintegration does not take place because each interest group sees benefits in abiding by the integrative process and penalties in abandoning it. There is a procedural consensus among the majority of the interest groups, and their expectations and demands are channelled towards integration. This is reinforced by the existence and the activities of the E.E.C. Commission which is a central co-ordinating body and which the pressure groups do not wish to offend even if their attitudes towards it may be sometimes negative. Thus the entire decision-making apparatus is biased towards integration. In Haas's words: 'The decision-making process, in its institutional setting, stimulates interest groups to make themselves heard and political parties to work out common positions; it creates pressure on high national civil servants to get to know and to establish rapport with their opposite numbers; and it sharpens the sensitivities of the legal profession.'[8]

Plausibly, the analysis postulates that, as pressure groups gain from the process of integration, they are stimulated to urge that the process be intensified. More arguably, it postulates that they are in a position to bring sufficient power to bear upon their national governments to make further integration unavoidable.[9] Haas may not be paying sufficient attention to vested national interests inherent in national governments and bureaucracies and to the fact that national values in the process of integration cannot be taken as constants; they can fluctuate and play a crucial role in reversing the integration process, as happened in 1965. Haas, however, who views the institutional and pressure-group activity as an intervening variable between economic and political integration, claims that the process of 'politicization' inexorably leads to complete supranational unification: 'The progression from a politically inspired Common Market to an eonomic union, and finally to a political union among states, is automatic.[10]

Haas's original dogmatic creed[11] is criticized by Stanley Hoffmann who refines and broadens the analysis. First of all, he distinguishes between 'high' and 'low' politics and claims that the decision—and hence the integration—processes fundamentally differ in the two domains. In low politics, concerned mainly with welfare economics (e.g. abolition of tariff barriers, raising of standards of living, etc.) integration can show a surplus of gains over losses and States will be prepared to countenance increased integration and even some shift in the focus of loyalties. When, however, we are concerned with high politics, concerning the ways of integrating the varying national concepts of physical defence and of defining the world role of the newly integrating grouping, disagreements are likely to arise and to obstruct political unification. Here the argument rests as the obvious example of de Gaulle's attitude is ambiguous. He showed that opposed trends based in low and in high politics can co-exist, however uneasily, and that disagreements on political decisions can disrupt the progress of high-level political integration without destroying continuing low-level integration. One cannot be sure in what way the clash will be reconciled but it seems plausible to guess that there is some vague threshold up to which the integration process will progress more or less automatically, although by no means uninterruptedly, as occasional setbacks must be expected. Beyond this threshold, a deliberate political decision is likely to be required. Theory cannot determine where the threshold will lie and whether a positive or negative decision will be taken to cross it but it can clarify the salient factors which are likely to play a part in determining both.

The other, broadening correction brought by Hoffman to Haas's somewhat oversimplified model is the general global setting in which regional integration is undertaken. As clearly demonstrated in the French–British differences on the British applications to enter the E.E.C., within the different historical experiences, backgrounds, values, and interests which have to be reconciled, the relationship with the outside world constitutes a crucial element. Hence it will be obviously difficult to agree about the world role of an enlarged E.E.C., especially about its relationship with the United States.

Finally, the integration theory has sufficiently advanced to appreciate that the conditions in the various regions in which the issue of integration exists may be so different as to demand a different model for adequate analysis. For instance, while the distinction between 'high' and 'low' politics is a useful concept in application to Western Europe, in the analysis of Gunnar Myrdal[12] the great discrepancies in economic development in other regions which result in excessive benefits for the more highly developed States, as well as the top priority accorded to economic growth, often mean that welfare politics, low in the European setting, become high politics in areas like East Africa or Latin America where they have effectively hampered progress towards integration.

4. THE PRESENT STATE OF THE INTEGRATION THEORY

The present state of the integration theory is authoritatively stated by its major proponent, Ernst B. Haas, in his review article 'The study of Regional Integration: Reflections on the Joy and Anguish of Pretheorizing' written in 1969. This serves as the basis for this section which refers also to a few of the additional nine articles elaborating some of the general themes and sketching out a few new areas for investigation, published in the Autumn 1970 special issue of the periodical *International Organisation*. Further work is, of course, in progress. Haas's article fully reflects the great strides the integration theory has made during the last fifteen years. While the theoreticians are still divided about the very definition of the concept they are studying, and often unclear about their assumptions, they have arrived at a whole series of empirical generalizations about integration in general, within the socialist groupings, in Western Europe, and in new States. The generalizations quoted concerning Western Europe show clearly how realistic the propositions are and also how far the theory has progressed from the rather naïve theorizing of the early functionalists; they are about Western Europe as it is now, taking

into full account the reversals of the integration process caused
by de Gaulle.

(*a*) Self-interest among governments and private groups has
sufficed to weave webs and expectations of interdependence and
mutual benefits. However, with shifts in economic conditions or in
the political climate these expectations are capable of being re-
versed and re-evaluated by the actors. Instrumental motives are
not necessarily strongly or permanently tied to the E.E.C.

(*b*) Collective decisions—from coal to steel, to tariffs on re-
frigerators, to chickens, and to cheese, and from there to company
law, turnover taxes, and the control of the business cycle—were
made incrementally, based often on consequences not initially intended by the actors (governments and important interest groups).
This tendency is summed up in the phrase 'spillover in the scope
of collective action'.[13]

(*c*) Spillover in scope is confined to decisions and objectives
relating to the realization of full benefits from an existing common market. It has operated markedly in free trade areas; nor has
it been true of all policy or decision sectors in common markets
(e.g. energy policy, transport).

(*d*) There has been very little spillover in the level of action,
i.e. little progressive penetration from supranational institutions
into the lower reaches of decision-making at the national and
local levels (with the exception of the mining and agricultural
sectors).

(*e*) Nevertheless, groups, contacts, and organizations (trade
unions, trade associations, working parties of civil servants, parliamentarians, students, professions) grow and prosper across fron-
tiers.

(*f*) The style of bargaining is incremental, subdued, and un-
emotional and seeks reciprocity of benefits, unanimous agreement,
and package deals among issue areas. French behaviour to the
contrary has not been accepted as legitimate and has not remained
fixed or final.

(*g*) Collective decisions with an economic substance tend to
exhibit most spillover characteristics when they are mediated by
a group of actors with overt or tacit federalist objectives. The pace
of integration slows down when this group is lacking, i.e. the
E.E.C. after 1963, the European Free Trade Association (EFTA).

(*h*) Young people in Europe are consistently more favourable to the intensification of the integration process than are older people in part because they are self-consciously non-nationalistic.

(*i*) The higher educated and professional layers of the population, of all ages, are consistently in favour of intensified integration. Those most satisfied with their standard of living also tend to favour integration. In short, pro-integration attitudes characterize the most successful and most 'modern' segments of the population.[14]

(*j*) A region of great cultural/linguistic homogeneity, even though its members easily create new ties between themselves, does not necessarily proceed easily to the making of integrative collective decisions when the issues perceived as being most salient by actors involve interdependence with countries outside the region. Hence self-encapsulation easily sets in with respect to practices and organs created previously (e.g. the Nordic Council and the network of Nordic co-operation).

The ultimate outcome of integration remains unclear and there is no full agreement about the definition of the independent variables and of their relationship, which greatly depends upon the theoretical framework chosen. Haas discusses three leading schools: federalism, communication theory, and neo-functionalism. Every one of these approaches starts with different assumptions and employs its own methodology. 'The federal approach assumes the identity of political postulates concerning common purposes and common need among actors irrespective of the level of action. It also assumes transferability, again on the basis of identical postulates, from the national to the regional level.' 'The communication approach proceeds on the basis of the logic of isomorphisms.' It uses the volume of transactions as its main indicator and it heavily relies upon aggregate and survey data. 'The neo-functionalist approach resorts to an extended analogy rather than relying on isomorphisms or identities between phenomena.' It assumes that postulates of actor perception and behaviour obtaining at the national level in pluralist Western societies apply also to the regional level; it heavily relies upon case-studies. The last two schools overlap. As these approaches do not offer fully fledged general theories of integration but merely enable us to proceed more systematically with the analysis of reality and to choose and classify the evidence available they are, in conformity with the present fashion, referred to as 'pre-theories'.

The research inspired by these 'pre-theories' is 'non-additive' and attempts to combine the findings are often as inconclusive as the proverbial one of adding apples and oranges; also the many empirical studies are at different levels of abstraction, bedevilling evaluation and comparison. One major difficulty is the lack of agreement about the nature of the end-product or 'dependent variable' which the theoreticians attempt to explain or predict. The federalists are clear but restricted in postulating a federal union; the communication theorists think of a 'security community' as a terminal condition, recognizing the possibility that it may be of an 'amalgamated' or 'pluralistic' variety; the neo-functionalists work with the idea of a political community or political union. The theoreticians are now aware of the confusion arising from their tendency to mix the imputed characteristic of the postulated dependent variable with those of independent or intervening variables.

While, in most cases, the terminal states originally envisaged in the various attempts at regional organization were fairly clear, they became greatly attenuated in the evolution of the actual institutions, rendering analyses based upon the original 'ideal types' rather remote from reality. One way out is to abandon the very idea of a defined end-state but to specify instead separate dimensions or conditions of integration which would constitute a higher degree of integration as compared to a previous point of time. In such an analysis the 'end-state' is a quantitatively specified point on a scale; when several salient dimensions are represented by separate scales, the end state is a specified convergence of separate curves. A purely theoretical high score on several dimensions is not, however, very meaningful, except in relation to the postulated task. Hence Haas fully approves of the categories developed by Leon Lindberg and Stuart Scheingold, positing three possible outcomes: fulfilment of the postulated task, retraction (i.e. distintegration), and extension. All the independent variables can be summed up and interpreted into recurrent patterns towards one of these outcomes.

As various organizations have different postulated tasks, we need a master concept which would adequately summarize and comprise all such tasks and would, moreover, enable us to provide scores indicating the direction in which the organization is going. Earlier analyses tended to focus upon élite loyalties but

Haas now proposes to concentrate upon the notion of 'authority–legitimacy transfer'. For both concepts ('authority' and 'legitimacy') it is possible to find specific indicators of universal validity, e.g. the notion of 'institutionalization'.

All these concepts do not amount to a new definition of a dependent variable but are helpful in evaluating the process at a somewhat higher level of abstraction than that of mere isolated hypotheses. Nor are they exhaustive, as we can visualize other outcomes, involving a higher degree of unity among the participating units. Haas proposes three illustrations of possible contemporary trends in this direction, differentiated by the degree to which legitimate authority is diffused: 'regional state', 'regional commune', and 'asymmetrical regional overlap'.

A regional state is a hierarchically ordered arrangement of the familiar State type with centralized authority marshalling and distributing resources, which is legitimate in the eyes of the individuals and of the subordinate structures on the basis of a kind of 'regional nationalism'. More unfamiliar would be a regional commune of interdependent units without a clearly defined centre of authority, as authority having been taken away from the previous centres has not found a new single focus. Legitimacy, however, it may be conceived, would not take the form of a loyalty of a nationalistic type. Asymmetrical overlapping is even more complex as the pattern of interdependence is asymmetrical—authority is withdrawn from the original units but is not proportionately or symmetrically vested in a new centre but is asymmetrically distributed among several. Although the ensembles would enjoy legitimacy in the eyes of the citizens, this legitimacy has no single focus; the image of infinitely tiered multiple loyalties may be appropriate. This image is based upon the evolving patterns in Western Europe.

The relevance of all this speculation becomes obvious when we turn to the problems of empirical investigation. Obviously we must seek some order and reduce the number of relevant independent variables or 'facts'. The techniques such as 'factor' or 'cluster' analysis are readily available and, indeed, some comprehensive and advanced schemes have been already proposed. This is and can be done only on the basis of the pre-theories which enable us to link the independent variables into some sort of an explanatory scheme and to use appropriately scored concepts associated with the explanation of one of the postulated outcomes to outline an action path towards it. Variables such as élites complementarity, perceived benefits from transactions, the role of external pressure, the substitutions of one type of leadership for another, and the creation of new groups of actors are obviously relevant; particular experiences are summed up by such empirically grounded evaluations as spillover, spill-around, institutionalization, élite responsiveness, learning, socialization. Thus evaluation of complex processes becomes possible.

Integration theory has still to develop the appropriate methods for tackling some central problems. First, whether the forces explaining the initiation of integration can be assumed to assure also its maintenance; second, how to analyse the apparent lack of congruence of national and regional styles; third, the degree to which developing countries deviate from the models evolved in the industrialized Western European context; fourthly, how to evaluate the links between transactions and attitude changes—how valid is the simple model which postulates a process of arriving at eventual trust through progressively more rewarding experiences.

Methodologically, integration theory is now as sophisticated as any international theory. To use some examples from the quoted volume of *International Organisation*, Leon N. Lindberg analyses 'Political Integration as a Multidimensional Phenomenon Requiring Multivariate Measurement'. This extensive and rigorous analysis of the evolution of collective decision-making is a great advance on old-fashioned analyses of 'supranational powers', as these powers are convincingly broken down into attributed power and prestige, a treaty-granting 'power' of initiative, and mastery of technical expertise. Donald J. Puchala brings balanced judgement upon the relevance of international transactions for regional integration by claiming that they are important but that their importance is limited to specific fields. He suggests convincing methods for measuring the flow of transactions. In 'Comparing Common Markets: a Revised Neo-Functionalist Model' J. S. Nye graphically represents the great advance and the increasing sophistication of this approach. The basic contemporary method is best summarized by Philippe C. Schmitter in 'A Revised Theory of Regional Integration'; the new theoreticians avoid wasting time on trying to isolate bivariate relations and on debating the relative merits of different (often equally arbitrary) measures; they reject macro-theories based upon single case-studies and upon idio-syncratic variables. Finally, Stuart S. Scheingold's brief summary of 'Domestic and International Consequences of Regional Integra-tion' shows how a theoretical analysis helps simplify and clarify attempts at a comprehensive evaluation which have, at least so far, been so inefficient in the E.E.C. debate in Britain.

5
The Actions of States

1. THE DECISION-MAKING APPROACH

A FULL theoretical analysis of decisions cannot be conceived except on the basis of a general theory of political behaviour. For that we have to determine three things: first, the rules governing the shift and the persistence of attention on the particular issues that occupy the political arena (often described as 'salience'); second, the principles governing the invention or design of potential courses of political actions; and, third, the rules which govern the choice of particular actions. Despite the efforts of the many scholars active in the field, progress towards a general theory has been insubstantial.

The decision-making approach to the analysis of foreign policy was pioneered by Professor R. C. Snyder and his associates in 1954.[1] Its basic assumption is that international action can be defined as sets of decisions made by recognizable units, that States behave as 'actors in a situation' and that within them, it is possible to identify 'decision-makers' whose 'authoritative acts are to all intents and purposes the acts of the State'. The authors identify the main forces influencing the decision-makers by classifying a wide range of factors within the external and the internal settings. The decision-making process is broken down into three subcategories:

(1) 'spheres of competence'—the activities of the decision-makers necessary for the achievement of the unit's objctives;
(2) 'communication and information'—meanings, values, and preferences available at the time of decision; and

(3) 'motivation'—psychological, personality, and value factors that influence the actors, enter the process, and influence its outcome. (See Diagram III.) All the roles, norms, goals, functions, and perceptions of the governmental organization in general as well as of the specific decision-making unit which is the subject of analysis can be neatly docketed and classified under the scheme which has, justifiably, been acclaimed as a major advance towards a systematic collection of data and as a basis for comparisons. The authors firmly belong to the school of 'cognitive behaviourists'; using the insights of individual and social psychology as well as of sociology, they enable us to explore in depth and with a degree of precision the whole decision-making process.

The major weakness of the approach is that it concentrates exclusively upon images and perceptions and ignores the objective reality which these reflect. The decisions are, however, implemented in the environment as it really is, and not as it is perceived; the 'feedback' process from it must not be neglected and it is important for us to measure the degree of congruence between reality and the perceptions of the élite, hence two parallel concepts can be introduced—of 'psychological environment' (images, perceptions) within which decisions are conceived, and of 'oper-

DIAGRAM III. A dynamic response model of a political system

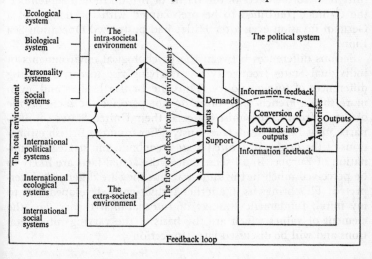

ational environment' within which foreign policy is executed.[2] The psychological environment determines the limits of possible decisions whereas the operational environment determines the limits of possible actions. The two environments do not necessarily coincide. The decision-maker may believe that there are opportunities for effective action which do not in fact exist, in which case his psychological environment is broader than his operational one; he may likewise ignore existing possibilities, thus narrowing his psychological environment in relation to the operational one. He may also do both consecutively, as a result of unexpected successes or of disappointed expectations, or even simultaneously, in different sectors of the environment. Each environment should be studied separately and they should be compared also with the psychological environments of other States in interaction with ours. Clearly discrepancies can be of crucial importance—compare, for instance, the nightmares of the early nuclear strategists fearing a surprise attack, when the missiles actually flying in the operational environment had not yet reached the decision-makers' psychological one. To take some actual historical examples: according to the previews of the contents of Government archives for 1940 released on January 1971, the non-existent Soviet menace was the dominant factor in the psychological environment of the Cabinet in 1940; likewise, not having fully realized the effect of the Battle of Britain in mid-September, the Cabinet continued to be preoccupied with the danger of a German invasion even after Hitler had postponed Operation Sea Lion.

Serious differences between the psychological environments of individual States frequently occur, giving rise to corresponding differences of foreign policy. Thus the British leaders and, even more so the French ones, often do not perceive the same degree of threat from Communist States as their United States counterparts; most French leaders seriously differ from the British estimations of the degree of United States economic and strategic domination of Europe. In all these States, the actual facts are likely to be perceived much in the same way but they are differently interpreted. This brings us to another insufficiently developed, but to my mind, fundamental aspect of international theory, i.e., the element of values which are the basis of the varying interpretations and will be discussed later, in section 5.

Somewhat related is the fact that the theorists rather unrealistically focus upon one actor whereas in real life this actor's decisions are invariably taken in interaction with other actors. Therefore the decision-making analysis seems to bear a similar relationship to the flow of decisions in real life—which is the subject-matter of other approaches discussed in the subsequent chapters—as film stills have to the whole film. Without enabling us to judge the flow of action as a whole they are helpful in the analysis of the details of acting and staging.

The term 'decision-making' has become part of the political vocabulary not only among scholars but also among politicians and journalists.[3] Many works have appeared which deal with some aspects of decision-making, although frequently without employing Snyder's elaborate framework or referring to all his extensive categories. This is understandable, as the number of variables distinguished by Snyder is overwhelming; a project following the scheme would have to process an enormous quantity of data and would, moreover, still remain deficient on the data which proved non-researchable. The inordinate complexity of the scheme is discouraging but, even more important, no theory of decision-making has emerged so that we remain unclear about the relations between the many variables. In fact, what the approach has produced amounts to little more than the setting out of categories which tells the researcher what data to collect and how to classify them but not how to use them. Despite the enormous investment of effort, few testable hypotheses have emerged. The main reason for this seems to lie in the fact that the scheme elaborates organizational variables but merely identifies those in the internal and external environments, while, obviously, the stimuli coming from these environments are an essential element in any theorizing about how decisions are made. To predict the direction, timing, and nature of political decisions we must interrelate the relevant variables pertaining not only to the actors but also to the targets of decisions and to the relationships between targets and actions. Only one significant case study following the scheme has been produced—that of the Korean conflict.[4]

The essence of foreign policy being the control of the external environment, either maintaining what we like or modifying what is undesirable in it or limiting the State's necessary adaptation to acceptable limits, concentration on the decision-making processes merely helps us to understand the mechanics but does not provide a satisfactory explanation of the broader aspects of foreign policy which is generally understood to consist of a series of responses to the changes in the environment. An attempt was made to include the concept of 'by-effects' or unexpected consequences of decisions but nobody has yet managed to structure the concept of a 'feedback' to indicate how such by-effects affect a foreign policy process in its course; it is merely an analytical term for a *post-mortem* analysis, relevant for subsequent decisions.

The decision-making approach has made a real contribution to the understanding of foreign policy processes by providing a new focus of interest to replace and supplement the traditional approaches, particularly those centring on power and equilibrium, or geopolitics, which had become increasingly less satisfactory and more sterile. It had the unfortunate effect of reinforcing the traditional distinction between domestic and international politics and, by the undue concentration upon the foreign policies of single States, it often detracted from a sustained effort to understand the broader processes of international interaction.

There is a considerable amount of literature about 'decision-theory', much of it related to business decisions, some of it mathematically formulated. Whereas, however, it is possible to produce quite plausible theorems about decision-making in business where we can safely assume that the decisions are rational within the concept of 'maximizing' or at least 'satisficing' (i.e. producing the minimum necessary) profits which can be calculated in monetary terms, no such calculations are possible for foreign policy. Here the psychological and emotional factors dominate and, owing to the uncertainty of information, a clear calculation even of the quantifiable elements is frequently impossible or of doubtful validity. Hence the assumption of rationality which is convenient for a neat theory, and, indeed for any deliberate clear-cut actual decision, cannot be taken for granted, and the problem whether rationality can be assumed is of fundamental importance for any theory or model.[5]

2. TYPES OF DECISION-MAKING APPROACH

An essential part of any theory is clear classification of its subject-matter into subdivisions about which it is possible to make more precise propositions than about the class as a whole. Thus, although the decision-making process is continuous and frequently confused, for analytical purposes, it is possible to distinguish stages—the pre-decisional one, the stage of choice, and the post-decisional one.[6] The decisions themselves can be divided into those which lead to action and those which do not; into initial and sequential decisions; according to the authority responsible ('executive' or 'legislative' or 'judicial'): according to the prevalence of domestic or foreign influence; perhaps most importantly, according to their crisis or routine nature or by their importance and urgency.

Among the many attempts to analyse the typology of decisions, only two will be discussed here. The first one proposed by David Braybrooke and Charles E. Lindblom[7] is ingenious and has been influential. It divides decisions according to two continua—one according to the degree of change sought, the other one according to the degree of information—between the extreme of a well-understood situation and one in which information is generally lacking and the values involved are not clearly understood or reconciled. The resulting neat diagrammatical arrangement, as below, enables us to place an actual decision within one of the four ensuing quadrants:

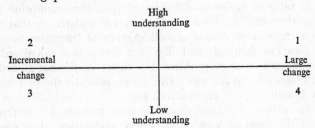

No historical examples can be found for quadrant 1 as the attempts to achieve large social changes are invariably based upon low rather than high understanding; the latter seems to be beyond our intellectual powers. To the examples quoted by Lindblom and Braybrooke of the decisions of the Southern States to secede and of the Soviet rulers to collectivize agriculture, could be added that of the British decision to join the European Communities— arguably higher on the axis of understanding but still in quadrant 4 rather than 1.

Whereas so far we have dealt with 'grand decisions', the remaining two quadrants encompass 'politics as usual.' We often attribute high understanding to some specialized 'expert' groups with recognized professional competence—administrators, military, economists, psychologists, etc. The basic idea of social sciences has traditionally been to break up intractable social problems into smaller, manageable segments, each of which can be dealt with by the appropriate 'experts' who can produce 'rational' decisions. Lately, however, grave doubts have started to arise in all political systems about the limitations of such procedures which tend to ignore broad, sometimes vital interests not falling within the limited expertise of the experts; the growing tendency to override the military in decisions on military procurement or the rejection of the Roskill Committee recommendations on a third London airport illustrate this trend.

The other, more recent analysis refers to the groups of conceptual models and the effect they can have upon the analysts and the practitioners applying them. Professor T. Allison proposed a scheme based upon a detailed investigation of the situation during the Cuban Missile Crisis.[8] He distinguishes three groups of models:

(1) *The rational policy model* is based upon the assumption that the government is the actor in a foreign policy situation; that each of its actions arises out of a well-formulated intention to meet some clear-cut demand; and that this action is a calculated response to some strategic problem. If a nation carries out an action, it must have an end for which this action provides the best means of attainment; out of alternatives, the one is chosen which is expected to achieve the most desirable consequences at a minimum cost, in the form of 'cost effectiveness' calculation. The Cuban 'quarantine' was the outcome of such calculations.

(2) *The organizational process model* sees the 'government' not as one unit but as a loosely co-ordinated group of semi-dependent organizations over which the leader may be able to exercise only partial control. The only way of acting is through standardized operational procedures. Hence governmental behaviour is not so much the deliberate choice of a leader as the output of large groups functioning according to their own standardized patterns of behaviour which provide the parameters of the leader's de-

cisions in any given situation. Therefore it may be difficult to adopt means suitable for dealing with a unique contingency. Applied to Cuba, this model explains the differences between the Air Force and the C.I.A. as to who should fly the U-2 aircraft which delayed the discovery of the missiles; the Navy's disobedience of the President's instructions about the location of the blockade line; the Navy's disagreement with the President as to why the Soviet ships were stopped.

(3) *The bureaucratic political model* interprets governmental behaviour as the result of political manoeuvring. Governments are seen as being composed of individuals each of whom possesses considerable discretion; power within the country is shared and the actual decisions depend upon the power, skill, and position of the politicians concerned. Action is not, therefore, necessarily the rational outcome of intentions but rather a compromise between differing points of views as it would be unrealistic not to assume that the separate individuals differ in their views and intentions. In the Cuban situation this illustrates the differences between the members of the presidential staff, the Chiefs of the Armed Forces, and C.I.A., and the difficulty with which these differences were reconciled.

The interesting aspect of this analysis is that it distinguishes the three models not as alternatives but as three complementary ways of analysis. Once the memoirs of Macmillan and Wilson are supplemented by additional inside information, we will be able to apply all three models to analyse the successive decisions to apply for membership of the E.E.C. taken by their respective governments.

3. THE STRATEGIC IMAGE

Any analysis of decision-making distinguishes between the cognitive and the affective components. The cognitive aspect describes the information that penetrates our cognition from the environment, but, as we perceive only a small fraction of reality, our knowledge of the environment is so limited and so personal that instead of speaking of 'knowledge' we generally refer to the 'image' or to 'the definition of the situation'.

These concepts apply only to the decision-makers or to the

informed and 'attentive' public. Theory is undecided about how to conceptualize the role of public opinion at large which, as most writers agree, exercises some constraints upon the conduct of foreign policy, especially in the democracies in which it sways the outcomes of elections. The early theory advanced by Gabriel Almond about the United States, centred upon the concept of 'moods', defined as unstable, fluctuating support for foreign commitments reflecting the low and unstable attention of the public to foreign affairs. Recent critics have, however, pointed out that the moods are generally stable and permissive. The way the American public tolerated the long involvement in Vietnam and then suddenly rebelled against it offers scope for a reformulation of the theory. Once the patterns of British attitudes towards the E.E.C. can be seen from the perspective of a few years after the proposed entry, the theory can be further developed.

If it is easy to misperceive objects or actions it is even easier to misperceive intentions. In fact, some political scientists have tried to advance hypotheses about misperceptions and have, for instance, formulated 'spiral theories' about the outbreaks of the 1914–18 War (Holsti, North, and Brodie) as well as the Cold War (Osgood, Etzioni, Boulding, and Singer). Evidence both from history and from psychology overwhelmingly supports the view that decision-makers fit incoming information into their existing theories and images; this happens in natural sciences, too. Our inclination to form balanced cognitive structures (discussed in the following section) leads to thinking which does not follow logical canons. It does not always amount to cognitive distortion as evidence is generally incomplete and wishful thinking does not perhaps occur quite as frequently as we sometimes suspect, but the whole process is not coherent and mutual misperceptions can have a cumulative effect, often ending in a conflict; quite a number of hypotheses have been formulated about misperceptions.[9]

On the whole, images are regarded as dependent variables but occasionally they are treated as independent ones, e.g. in an analysis of Norwegian foreign policy by Philip M. Burgess[10] whose concept of 'strategic image' is followed here. The cognitive component of a strategic image refers to the decision-maker's view and definition of the central features of the international environment (his perception); the affective (emotional and volitional) component refers to the valuational dimension of the image structure, the way he assigns his likes and dislikes, his approval and disapproval of these conditions. To some extent, the affective component overlaps the cognitive one as it acts as a sort of a filter in determining our evaluation of the importance and relevance of the things observed; thus, in a way, it also determines what we actually perceive because it fits into our image and what we ignore because it does not.

Thus the term 'strategic image' summarizes the way in which a policy-maker organizes, structures, evaluates, and relates to his environment. Some images are more 'open', i.e. susceptible to modification or revision through feedback than others, but one of the major characteristics of all images is a relative stability over time. Major changes in strategic images arise through traumatic experiences or through changes of personnel, e.g., Hitler's occupation of the rump of Czechoslovakia altered Chamberlain's image of Hitler, but a more thorough transformation of the British national image of Hitler came later and was expressed by the change of personnel when Churchill became the Prime Minister.

The strategic image performs an integrating function by allowing its holder to make sense of, and thereby organize and integrate, the information he receives; it has also an orienting function through clarifying expectations about the future. If we determine the strategic images of the main policy-makers rather than those of the attentive or expressive public and work out the dynamics of the change of this image across time, we have a useful tool for 'negative prediction', that is, of courses of actions that will not be selected, of alternatives that will not be chosen or even explored or considered. De Gaulle, for instance, had a clear notion that the strategic image of Britain hinged on the 'special relationship' and that Britain would not do anything to upset it. He was right in claiming that Macmillan's conversion to Europe was not really based upon a change in this image, but was, in all likelihood, wrong in thinking the same about Wilson. Mr. Pompidou's initial hesitation about the third British application may be plausibly expressed in terms of uncertainty about the degree of change of the British strategic image; this, of course, cannot be considered as a full explanation of his tactics.

The concept may also prove to have fair explanatory powers, as what seems 'irrational' in itself may appear to be quite consistent with it and therefore rational when viewed within the frame-

work of the strategic image. Thus the accumulation of hard knowledge by a rigorous and reliable elaboration of the strategic images
of other national élites and aspiring élites may be a useful policy
tool. Of course, the connection between strategic images and policy
outcomes may greatly vary from country to country, from time to
time and, possibly, within different issue areas; it may, however,
be possible to find out in very general terms the way they mediate.

Common sense indicates that a systematic understanding of
others' strategic images is the only sound foundation of diplomacy.
Moreover, improving and rendering more favourable the images
others hold of us presents a promising instrument for exercising influence in the world. Some psychological theorists claim that the
improvement of one's image in others' eyes is the only promising
modern way of exercising influence, superior to the traditional
ones of using economic and military power. This claim seems
greatly exaggerated but less so today than it was a quarter of a
century ago. Anyway, although we are never quite sure about the
effects of propaganda and information services, these seem to be
easier to calculate than those of the traditional economic and
strategic instruments.

4. THE CONSISTENCY THEORY

One of the most striking characteristics of images is their tendency to be consistent and durable. These characteristics are the
subject of a whole group of closely related explanations which are
loosely labelled as 'consistency theory'. All the variants conceive
attitudes or constellations of attitudes to be organized according
to some internal order—'balance', or 'consonance'—which is
homeostatic, i.e. self-adjusting. A substantive disturbance of the
order renders it unstable and generates symbolic activity in order
to re-establish the balance. Therefore, according to their impact
upon the order—or as it has been termed in the preceding section
the 'strategic image'—elements of reality can be classified as positive, negative, or neutral.

Three major models have been proposed in this approach. The
best-known is Festinger's theory of cognitive dissonance to which
is attached a rather loose school based upon the hypothesis that
a person holding two inconsistent cognitions will be motivated to
remove the dissonance; the congruity model deals with the im-

pacts of certain types of information and claims that they result in determinate changes of attitudes; the balance model is similar but less specific in its prediction. The meaning and uses of these models can be illustrated by their application to the study of British Labour Party members. Whereas the vaguer balance model is appropriate to the study of the attitudes of the non-parliamentarians as these are less articulate and hence less open to stricter analysis, the attitudes of Labour parliamentarians can be studied by the congruity model.

The generally accepted division of the Labour supporters into Fundamentalist Left and Revisionist Right largely coincides with a polarization of attitudes to Germany ranging from pathological hatred to a complete acceptance as an international partner; this attitude seems to be the major determination of attitudes to the E.E.C. The election of Herr Brandt as the German Chancellor created a clearly 'negative element' for the extreme Fundamentalist who basically suspects Germany. His main strategy for trying to re-establish congruence is incredulity, simply claiming that Herr Brandt is a socialist only in name; he may shift his position but, according to the model, being extreme, he moves only little. By contrast, a considerably less anti-German Revisionist finds it much easier to re-evaluate his appraisal of Germany. Although the attempts made to quantify the attitudes are not impressive, the graphic as well as the verbal analysis of the process is very clear.

In the less ambitious balance model we do not attempt to quantify positions but merely define them with a sign—positive, negative, or null. The model postulates that equilibrium obtains if objects of identical sign are linked by positive or null bonds, or objects of different signs are linked by negative or null bonds. When a clash of values occurs, there exist three major methods of adjustment:

(1) to change the sign of one or more objects or of the bond linking them;
(2) to differentiate, i.e. split the object into various parts and select the part that contributes to the balance;
(3) to cease thinking about the matter.

To return to our Labour Party members and their attitudes to 'three grand circles', a Fundamentalist with a positive attitude to the New Commonwealth and a negative one to the E.E.C. is in equilibrium; a Revisionist may try to upset the Fundamentalist's equilibrium by suggesting that this negative attitude leads to the detriment of the New Commonwealth as the associated ex-French colonies compete with it. The Fundamentalist may correct the imbalance either by ignoring the argument or by differentiating and changing the sign (meaning adopting a positive attitude) to the Associated States, claiming that they share interests with the New Commonwealth and it is merely the colonialist forces of the E.E.C. that operate to the latter's detriment. The Revisionist, however, will try to persuade the Fundamentalist to change the sign (meaning change the attitude to a positive one) to the whole E.E.C., re-evaluating it as a contributor not only to the Associated States but also, potentially, to the New Commonwealth.

A Revisionist can be in an equilibrium by evaluating all the three circles positively. The Fundamentalist who wishes to convert him will attack the positive linkage sign, claiming that many Commonwealth leaders are strongly opposed both to the United States and the E.E.C.; his ideal final equilibrium would incorporate also the conviction that the United States is using the E.E.C. for the purposes of the Cold War. Thus, from an initial equilibrium of three positive attitudes with null or positive links, the converted Revisionist would retain a positive attitude only to the New Commonwealth but he would adopt a negative one both to the United States and to the E.E.C. so that positive links between the opposed elements would be precluded.

5. VALUES AND THE NATIONAL INTEREST[11]

Although everybody agrees about the central role that values and interests play in foreign policy, these are such fundamental notions that they defy definition by reference to other terms. Values describe the inner element brought to bear by the decision-makers upon the processes of making decisions. It is analytically convenient although often empirically impossible to determine whether the values found in the formulation of a specific interest had been internalized by the decision-makers or introduced only in response to environmental pressures, generally domestic but sometimes also international.

Little agreement can be reached on the nature and the significance of this element and many overlapping and ill-defined terms are employed to denote it: ideologies, doctrines, values and valuations, aspirations, utilities, policies, commitments, goals, objectives, purposes, ends, programmes, ethos, the way of life, etc., etc. The distinctions proposed are generally unconvincing. Our understanding in inhibited by social taboos arising from the desire to preserve the national value system from cold rational scrutiny which would expose its inconsistencies and weaken its emotional impact, as well as by the difficulties of analysis. Confusion arises also from the complex ends–means relationships in which values can be frequently regarded as ends in themselves but also as means for other values. Thus in his recent book *Britain in Tomorrow's World* (1969) Hugo Grant distinguishes between 'aspirations' and 'interests' and claims that joining Europe is indicated by the latter though rejected by the former. It seems more penetrating to go to a deeper level and to start with Britain's fundamental desire to retain as much independence and to exercise as much influence as is possible for her in today's—or tomorrow's—world. Joining the E.E.C. is clearly an instrumentality—according to many people the only promising instrumentality—towards these fundamental aspirations. Hence to state that British aspirations do not lie in Europe is misleading rather than illuminating; it is merely a description of our reluctance to use extremely unorthodox means.

However vague, controversial, and abused in political usage, the term 'national interest' is the most widely used and generally intelligible shorthand description of all the purposive elements in foreign policy. In the West, the idea of 'national interest', together with that of the 'nation', appears to be losing its supreme place in politics and, particularly in the E.E.C. context, can be regarded as an archaic obstacle to integration. It certainly still fully applies to many policies of its members, particularly of France. However, if Britain is to join the Community, surely a full understanding of what is involved in her own national interest does not, contrary to the prejudices of many critics of the concept, create an obstacle towards her integration. On the contrary, it is the only possible sound foundation for such integration. Especially as Mr. Heath has been frequently referring to the British 'national interest', it seems worth while to sketch out its analysis with references to Britain's problems.

The obvious interest of the confused concept which has been

so much abused in political usage, lies in its relationship with actual political behaviour. A relevant major analytical distinction is that between three levels on which the concept is used—the aspirational, the operational, and the polemical ones. The logic of this classification is imperfect as the third category overlaps with the first two; moreover, the categories suggested do not escape the nature of ideal types. Nevertheless the classification is operationally convenient as every single use of 'national interest' falls predominantly, though seldom exclusively, within one of the proposed categories.

On the aspirational level, 'national interest' refers to the vision of the good life, to some ideal set of goals which the state would like to realize if this were possible. If such 'national interest' is not actively pursued this does not mean that it is politically irrelevant, since, given an opportunity through favourable changes in the environment or in the power of the State, it may become operational. Thus while it would be a mistake to attribute an immediate operational significance to the professed Soviet desire to communize the world, it would be likewise a mistake to consider this desire as meaningless and incapable of becoming operational in some favourable circumstances. On the operational level, national interest refers to the sum total of interests and policies actually pursued. The main distinctions between the two levels are that aspirational interests are generally long-term, rooted in history and ideology, need not be fully articulated or co-ordinated, and can be contradictory; they are determined more by political will than by capabilities. Operational interests tend to be the very opposite. The interrelationship between the two levels is significant in determining political dynamism. Such dynamism is lacking in the extreme situations when aspirations are either clearly beyond any chance of achievement or pitched so low that they approximate to actual policies. Changes, whether in the power of the State or in the international environment, which affect the State's 'net achievement capability', i.e. its capacity to achieve its objectives, can seriously affect the distance between aspirations and policies since any revision of the contents of national interest need not take place simultaneously at both levels.

While the former two categories are purely analytical, the third, explanatory and polemical level refers to the use of the concept in political argument in real life, to explain, evaluate, rationalize, or criticize international behaviour. It is used less to describe or prescribe than to prove oneself right and one's opponents wrong. As a dominant proportion of political behaviour is verbal, argument is the most important source of information but its relations to non-verbal behaviour present great difficulties of analysis. The proposed distinctions can help to resolve some of them. When politicians say things different from what they are actually doing, they are not always guilty of hypocrisy and their statements are not meaningless. On the contrary, these statements always bear some relation both to aspirations and to the policies actually pursued and can be fruitfully analysed to explain the relationship between the two.

Within the limitations of space it is impossible to do more than outline some of the outstanding problems confronting us in the analysis of national interest. In the first instance there is a fundamental disagreement between those who conceive it broadly and hence vaguely and others who try to pin it down to a number of concrete elements, factors, dimensions, or functions. The former believe that any attempt to break down the concept is bound to leave out the essentials and would also give scope to the pursuit of sectional interests at the cost of the general good, as even the most hard-bitten pragmatists pursue some general theory—usually based upon selfish self-interests and, moreover, a rather poor one. They also believe in general philosophical analysis and often attach great importance to intuitive understanding. The latter endeavour to introduce a scientific method, and, in conformity with the trends of contemporary social science, to break down the intractable concept into meaningful and clearly defined elements.

Obviously it would be desirable to avoid either extreme and to achieve as scientific an approach as feasible without, at the same time, losing sight of national interest as a whole. The likely solution seems to lie in the employment of clearly defined models concentrating on a few dimensions selected as independent variables, leaving the other significant dimensions as constants. As long as such models are employed in the full awareness of their limitations, they need not blind us to national interest as a whole. The dangers of concentrating upon one such model are, however, great. Thus, for instance, in the perennial debates on 'guns or butter' which recur in all political systems, models of national interest defined either in predominantly economic or in predominantly strategic terms are widely employed but, even if scientifically rigorous, these are politically unconvincing. They cannot be reconciled except on the basis of a broader conception of national interest, incorporating both. Unfortunately the general theories of international relations do not supply a clue for our search for national interest as a whole. Only the power theory is explicit by postulating that national interest is defined by power, i.e., the capacity to continue national existence and to pursue national goals. As power is merely instrumental, however, the power theory is not very helpful for determining the ultimate contents of national interest.

Even without a clear framework for the classification of the dimensions of national interest it is well worth while to clarify as far as possible some of its important aspects. For instance, there is promise in the analysis of the scope of national interest which may embrace and synthesize the voluminous work on the relationship between domestic and foreign policies, on isolationism and involvement in world politics, on self-sufficiency and interdependence. The notion of 'vital interests' and their relationship to changes in the international environment are another fruitful aspect. Finally, to come down to Kant's basic categories of human thinking, the spatial and the time dimensions can be usefully investigated.

In relation to Britain's postwar foreign policy, some of the concepts evolved in the analysis can be useful. 'Salience' can be used to identify an obviously important but seldom fully recognized contributory reason for her failure to take an interest in Western European integration, i.e. her preoccupation with domestic issues such as the establishment of the Welfare State and nationalization as well as with imperial patterns which lie between the domestic and the foreign fields. The whole postwar argument about the main direction of British foreign policy, summed up by the 'grand three circles' metaphor, can be structured by defining the appropriate spatial scope of the British national interest. Gradually shedding the illusion that it could possibly remain world-wide despite Britain's diminished capabilities, the successive governments in their varying ways were moving towards the choice of the most relevant regional context which, for defence and later also economic reasons, could not be anything but West-

ern Europe. The fundamental problem of the limitation of
national sovereignty involved in joining the E.E.C. can be analysed 'dialectically' in terms of one of the several major dilemmas
facing modern States—that between autonomy and interdependence.

Finally, as Mr. Heath himself has repeatedly indicated, a
thorough clarification of Britain's national interests is now necessary; it seems essential to provide a rational basis for the current
fundamental reappraisal of Britain's foreign policy which, in a
simplified form, could be described as a shift of emphasis from
attempts at controlling the international environment to concentration upon adaptive behaviour, as analysed in chapter III, section 7. One of the major principles by which British foreign policy
has been traditionally governed is that of harmonization, as clas-
sically expressed by Sir Eyre Crowe and repeated in innumerable
official statements. The ideal of accommodation, of compromise,
the notion that these are much more useful than confrontation,
used to be the mainstay of the strength of Britain's diplomacy.
This was a profitable technique for the dominant Power. To give
only one example, the principle of 'free trade' not only made
British naval dominance more readily acceptable to others but
was also commercially advantageous to the country which had
industrialized first. This principle died during the Great Depres-
sion and, characteristically, after the last World War, it was no
longer Britain but the United States which became its main
champion.

In a broader sense, however, the idea lingered that Britain
should exert herself on behalf of the broadest 'milieu goals', that
she must be a major contributor to world order. Acting as a
'policeman' in regions of special interest was one of the reasons as
well as rationalizations for the heavy military expenditure East of
Suez. Only in the late sixties was this objective abandoned.

For obvious reasons, in her negotiations to enter the E.E.C.
the British Government has to accept the 'rules of the Community' although many of these have been shaped in a form dis-
regarding British interests in various fields and even opposed to
them; only a few exemptions and transitional arrangements are
actually negotiated. Obviously, if and when a member of the
Community, the British Government will have to harmonize its
policies with those of other members to an even greater degree,

and harmonize them not only in a context in which Britain is no longer dominant, but in one which has been shaped without any British contribution and without any regard for Britain's eventual entry, and shaped, moreover, very largely to suit the interests of France. Once Britain is in, she will obviously wish to adjust Community policies to conform as closely as possible with her own, individual interests. The tradition of harmonization will serve well the officials and politicans involved in the process of negotiations about any amendments or developments, but is it not possible that the substance and outcome of these negotiations may be so heavily weighted in favour of the Community as a whole, and of France who benefits most from it, that it may insufficiently accommodate Britain's own individual interests where they are at variance? Britain's traditional diplomatic style may prove fully suitable to the conditions within the Community and may, indeed, command greater support from others than the more antagonistic French style but is it not likely that, within the familiar and favourably shaped context, the French interests, whenever not conforming with ours, may usually prevail? The principle of harmonization works well for a dominant power but less so for one which is not dominant unless its Government is quite as clear as are all other parties about what its specific national interests are and also determined to pursue them. In the interests of the Community, it is obviously necessary for the members to resist selfish attitudes but, as the Germans have apparently lately started to realize, this need not be done to excess.

All this would be clear to all diplomatic and political personnel who may be involved but I very much doubt whether this awareness is sufficient to prevail unless backed by as full as possible clarification, not only of the specific individual interests which may come up but also of a much more general appreciation of Britain's national interest as a whole. The nineteenth-century tradition that Britain's interests would be served well in an orderly world can be readily transposed into the narrower context of the Community but the equation no longer holds—while an orderly development of the Community would be clearly in Britain's interest, once she is in, a full clarification of this national interest in a systematic way is the essential foundation for ensuring that important aspects of it are not neglected in the process. While the analysis of Britain's national interest is the necessary philosophical foundation, the actual operation within the Community can be usefully theoretically structured according to the theories dealing with the interaction of States, using the models of social communication and of bargaining. The models of a 'non-zero-sum-game' in which co-operation increases the sum total of benefits and those of 'bargaining' to ensure a 'fair' national share in the co-operative ventures are likely to be relevant. These models are discussed in the next chapter.

6. CONCEPTIONS OF 'ROLE'

Elements of decision-making as well as broad social considerations involved in state behaviour can be brought together in the analysis of national 'roles'.[12] Already in traditional theories, international roles were occasionally discussed as variables, e.g. in the balance-of-power theory the roles of an aggressor-state, of a group defending the *status quo*, and of a balancer. In the postwar world we talk of non-alignment or of Britain's world role. These notions are not, however, very frequent and the meaning of international 'role' requires clarification.

The concept of 'role' in general is well articulated in the social sciences, especially in sociology. Definitions vary but the concept generally refers to behaviour—to decisions and actions. Definitions of role are found both in the role prescription by others and in the actor's own conception of his position and function and of the behaviour appropriate for them. Sometimes the concept of 'status' can be used as an alternative. Role prescription in international politics is pronounced mainly within international organizations and is by no means uniform in each case. Thus the French and the British have quite different definitions of the appropriate behaviour for the members of NATO, and the anti-colonial members of the U.N. take a quite different view of the obligations of members administering non-self-governing territories from that of Britain and France.

The fact that States are sovereign means that the behaviour is determined mainly by their own role conception rather than through prescription by others. This conception includes the policy-makers' own definitions of the general kinds of decisions, commitments, rules, and actions suitable for their State, and of functions, if any, that the State should perform on a continuing basis within the international system or a subordinate regional system. The main sources of national role conceptions can be found in the location, resources, and capacities of the State, in its traditional policies, in socio-economic demands, needs at home, interest groups, national ideologies, moods, and personalities. Role prescriptions coming from the outside—world opinion, treaties, commitments, understandings, etc.—play only an indirect part in the State's own definitions.

The description of the main types of national roles in the theoretical literature is fairly vague. Within the many analyses of balance-of-power systems, the national roles, whether deliberately adopted or not, appear in a grossly simplified form. One major typology which was fashionable in the immediate postwar years was that coined by Professor Hans Morgenthau. According to him, national roles fall within three major categories according to whether the nation is intent primarily to keep power, to increase power, or to demonstrate power, leading to policies of *status quo*, imperialism, or prestige. Non-alignment cannot be accommodated in this terminology which concentrates upon power relations. In a broader setting, many writers distinguish three major continua which cut through one another: satisfied/dissatisfied, active/passive, and powerful/weak. Obviously different combinations of these three dimensions result in quite different types of foreign policy roles.

Finally, a distinction worth remembering is that between a first-rank Power which can exercise decisive influences upon world politics and to whom all the above categories fully apply, and second-rank Powers which are involved in world politics but are incapable of decisive influence and hence find their roles defined largely through their relations with the Powers of the first rank. Major second-rank roles distinguished are those of ally-mediator, *provocateur*, or independent.[13] Although the classification is not very elaborate, Professor Holsti's analysis of official statements by seventy-one States in the late sixties provides an interesting starting point for the comparison of various national conceptions of 'role'. To take the cases of Britain and France, we find no reference in Britain to the role of 'active independent', frequent in France, or to that of a 'regional leader', whereas the French do not refer to the category of 'regional protector' popular among the British leaders. 'Mediator/integrator' was the role the French most fre-

quently referred to, against that of 'regional subsystem collabor-
ator' in Britain; French references to the role of 'faithful ally' were
much less frequent than the British ones. None of these categories
adds substantially to the conventional wisdom about British and
French foreign policies but their analysis contributes to a more
systematic comparison of the two.

6

States in Interaction

1. PEACE RESEARCH

ALTHOUGH the behavioural study of States in action has moved far from the limitations of the traditional theories of power politics, it has not been fully able to shed its origins within these theories; thus, suggestions that 'national interest' should be analysed are met not only with the justified objection that it is extremely difficult to study but also with the unjustified one that it necessarily ties us to narrowly conceived power political State objectives. Moreover, the concentration of the decision-making analysis upon one State does not allow an easy comprehension of interaction with the environment. All this is well understood by the more enlightened theoreticians but is given a clearer expression in the so-called 'peace research' school. Peace researchers endeavour to persuade governments to follow the successes of natural sciences in 'solving problems' and to employ social sciences for finding similar solutions. Although they are frequently critical of governmental behaviour, with the growing *détente*, governments have begun to share with them interest in some phenomena, e.g. in arms control or in the avoidance of accidental wars.

'Peace research' is a highly motivated approach. It arises from the desire to abate conflict and to prevent war, often specifically to work for various forms of disarmament, to abolish weapons systems geared to mass destructions, to prohibit the more inhuman aspects of war, etc. 'Peace research' describes a common objective rather than a common school based upon a single method or group of methods. It is interdisciplinary research which is particularly favoured by the few natural scientists who have decided to launch a crusade against war and/or conflict and to work for their abolition, and also by some social scientists. It has flourished particularly in Canada, Norway, the Netherlands, but also in the United Kingdom. Although widespread among academics, it unites them not in their official capacities within universities but generally under the umbrella of special peace or conflict research institutes. It is organized in separate national units but has wide international links, including those with Communist countries, starting with the famous Pugwash Conferences. Its method is frequently quantitative; its substantive findings, many of which are published in the *Journal of Peace Research* and also in the *Journal of Conflict Resolution* can be referred to under the other headings of this chapter, especially those relating to the theories of conflict, of games, and of bargaining.

2. CONFLICT ANALYSIS[1]

The name 'theory of conflict' or 'conflict analysis' covers many heterogenous schools and approaches, some motivated by the search for peace, others by the desire to improve the performance of a State's external policies, and others again by the mere search for understanding. They comprise sociological, philosophical, and ethical analyses of the nature of conflict and, often separately, of violent conflict and war, schools of conflict management and of conflict resolution, and the various schools with more specific techniques or subjects, some of which are discussed in subsequent sections. This one deals with only a few general themes.

Although some writers concentrate upon international conflicts alone and some of them only upon their violent subclass of war, the majority regard international conflict as a subclass of human conflicts in general and hence attempt to draw parallels from conflicts in settings other than the international one.

In simplest terms, a conflict exists when two people or groups of people, including States, wish to carry out acts which are mutually incompatible. In most situations, the parties can deliberately choose between pursuing this conflict and seeking some co-operative alternative which is often called 'conflict resolution.'

Not all national interests are, of course, incompatible with those of some other State and conflict is therefore avoidable if the appropriate interests are chosen and avoided. Thus the first level at which the issue of conflict resolution arises is that of determination of interests and of objectives. In the terminology of the late Professor A. Wolfers[2] goals can be divided into two dichotomous classes, 'possession goals' and 'milieu goals'. The essence of the former is to enhance or preserve things to which the State attaches value; they include anything—ranging from the control of territory, a seat in the Security Council, to tariff preferences. Their main characteristic is found in their competitive nature: the State demands a share of certain values which are in limited supply and this, inevitably, is at the cost of others, for which a *quid pro quo* can, of course be offered. This situation is described in the theory of games as a 'zero-sum-game'. The essence of 'milieu goals' is that they do not aim at the defence or increase of possessions held to the exclusion of others, but at shaping the conditions of the international environment. The main characteristic of such goals is that they are achieved not at the cost of but to the mutual benefit of others; they are based on a 'non-zero-sum' model of international politics. The stark contraposition of these two classes is often exaggerated in the political debates—the chauvinists are naturally concerned with exclusive national possessions while the internationalists regard these possessions as an expression of a reprehensible spirit of national selfishness and acquisitiveness; the former tend to reject and the latter tend to embrace rather indiscriminately all milieu goals.

The choice at this level is clearly important. If a State concentrates upon possession goals, inevitably it is drawn into conflict with other States whose wills must be overcome; if it concentrates upon mileu goals, it must secure the co-operation of other States without which the goals become unattainable. Suspicion of milieu goals extends to suspicion of co-operation, which, when concerning vital interests, may jeopardize the security and military preparedness of the State. The dilemmas of choice are often acute, as best shown by the difficulties of disarmament. The more a State concentrates upon the conflict type of interaction and amasses armaments, the less chance it has to proceed co-operatively towards a disarmament scheme. The more it concentrates upon co-operation and, to encourage it, reduces its military preparedness for acute conflict and for countering violence, the more it incapacitates itself for facing possible dire contingencies. In fact, no statesman can accept the stark dichotomy between the mode of conflict which is characteristic of the past systems of power politics and that of co-operation which, hopefully, is supposed to characterize the brighter future ahead. In the choice of his goals and of the means for their pursuit he is constantly forced to choose a combination of the two modes which, however, can significantly vary from nation to nation, and, within each nation, from government to government and from individual to individual.

The general attitudes adopted to conflict and co-operation give the decision-makers a sense of direction when they are faced with the choice of conflict or co-operation in specific issues. They decide according to how much value they attach to the principle of co-operation as well as to the various kinds of co-operation, and according to how much risk they are willing to take to wage conflicts in general and in their various forms. Needless to say, this general sense of direction falls far short of a complete and reliable guide to specific decisions. A short-cut constantly employed to avoid the obvious difficulties of carefully weighing the pros and cons of each issue is to form generally conceived relationships of friendship and hostility which, to a large extent, pre-determine the mode of interaction on all the issues which may arise. This short-cut carries its own dangers and dilemmas and merely simplifies the decision-makers' task. The assumptions of identity of interests with an alliance and of divergence of interests with the opposed bloc are not fully tenable, especially in the long run; the world does not readily divide into friends and foes, heroes and villains and, moreover, it constantly changes. The revaluation of what mode of interaction best serves the interests of the State is a constant and continuing process.

The following issues are frequently discussed in the analysis of conflict:

(1) The assumption is made that conflict takes place among parties which act rationally and are fully informed. Although realistically all the theoreticians know that this is an ideal type of situation which cannot ever be fully matched in real life, they have to make this assumption as calculations are otherwise impossible. To some extent, even within highly mathematical models, the uncertainties of information and of the irrational elements can be allowed for but rarely quite adequately. One of the major reser-

vations about the practical use of conflict resolution models relates to the lack of full information and the limitations of rationality in real life.

(2) The ideas about the social role of conflict vary. Some writers regard it as an aberration, 'deviant' or 'dysfunctional' behaviour even though its complete elimination appears to be utopian.[3]

Others (especially Georg Simmel or Lewis Coser) stress the role of conflict as a useful social device in containing within one system interests which are not fully compatible. Here a parallel—which obviously should not be stretched too far—can be drawn between social and biological organization. In order to ensure flexibility and to avoid dangerous overadaptation, both organisms and societies prefer to combine a flexible mix of two opposites to a straightforward arrangement—cf. male and female genes or hormones and anti-hormones on the one hand, and such dichotomies as freedom and authority or centralization and decentralization upon the other.

Specifically about international conflicts:

(3) Some enthusiasts of international organization tend to equate conflicts with the behaviour of States outside these organizations and co-operation with the behaviour of the States within them as well as the activities of the organizations themselves. Mercifully, some of the traditional behaviour of States is often co-operative, e.g. in the old-fashioned alliances; States do not necessarily behave co-operatively within international organizations, and the activities of the latter have so far been rather limited.

(4) International conflict is often rather facilely equated with violence and war and an unwarranted parallel is drawn with the progression of domestic political systems from violence to order, through the evolution of methods of adjustment and the enforcement of law. The hopefully expected evolution of the international system is, however, unlikely, as the alternatives to violence are lacking and the enforcement authority is non-existent. The fact that there seems to exist a firm international consensus upon avoiding an all-out nuclear war has not fundamentally altered the situation that violence is effectively used to resolve conflict situations.

(5) As conflicts arise in many forms and for many reasons, it is

generally misleading to generalize about their causes, e.g. to attribute them all to misperceptions and faulty social communication–
while some are thus caused, others are based upon real differences
of interest which, if more clearly realized, merely exacerbate the
conflict.

However[4] optimistic or pessimistic we may feel about the possibilities of conflict resolution, it behoves us to seek the most appropriate intellectual tools for analysing them. An important initial
step lies in an adequate classification of conflict situations and
here a commendable scheme proposed by Anatol Rapoport in
Fight, Games and Debates (1960) has become quite popular.

In a fight situation the opponent is merely a nuisance to be
eliminated, subjugated, cut down to size. Fundamental religious
and ideological conflicts come under this category, for example
the Arab–Israeli and Indian–Pakistani issues, as seen by many
nationals of these states.

In a game situation each opponent wishes to win at the cost of
his fellow but they co-operate within the rules of the game, in fact
they are essential for each other since otherwise, without the
opponent, there would be no game at all. The assumption under-
lying a game relationship is that the opponent is not a fiend to
be destroyed, but much like oneself, perhaps unpleasant and even
very dangerous, but essentially governed by the same basic rational
considerations. His possible and likely countermoves to one's own
moves can be rationally anticipated and hence one's own moves
should be devised accordingly. Many adherents of the 'theory of
games' have been assiduously applying it to international relations. Even in 'zero-sum games', where the outcome is fixed and
the share of one side must be carved out of that of the opponent,
the game sometimes allows a 'saddle-point' which, on the assumption of rational behaviour on both sides, allows the greatest possible benefit (or smallest possible loss) to both. In the more complex 'non-zero-sum games' a harmonious, co-operative play im-
proves the final outcome so that both sides can be better off. It
would be foolhardy to expect, as a few of the adherents of the
games theory do, that the theory will ever be directly applicable
to the resolution of actual conflict situations which are infinitely
more complex than game situations. Undoubtedly, however, the
theory of games sharpens our appreciation of real-life conflicts

and provides a readier frame of mind to tackle them co-operatively.

Finally in a debate situation, each participant reasons not only about the opponent's possible countermoves but endeavours to convince him, to obtain his consensus. This is actually a situation frequently encountered in international politics: it is the basis of inter-state negotiations as well as of some of the debates in the General Assembly of the United Nations. Thousands of international agreements are concluded every year; prolonged, laborious and acrimonious as General Assembly debates often are, even on such vast and controversial subjects as disarmament, human rights, and national self-determination they have resulted in a limited degree of effective persuasion embodied in some international agreements and declarations.

Conflict is not uniformly grave in all the various relations between any two states and hence the total behaviour of the two will never fall within one single class. To take the extreme of a 'fight' like World War II, even then both sides engaged in 'game' behaviour when trying to anticipate the likely countermoves of the adversary and refraining from the use of poison gas or the grossest forms of maltreatment of prisoners-of-war. On the other hand, such staunch allies as the United States and Great Britain during the period of an undoubted 'special relationship' in the War generally treated the issues on which they were in conflict as issues of 'debate'—they tried, admittedly sometimes unsuccessfully, to use persuasion, and 'fight' between them was unthinkable. When, however, their specific interests were clashing beyond the possibility of persuasion, they also employed 'game' tactics. This was the case with independence for British colonies, with spheres of interest in Eastern Europe, or with the question of the siting and timing of the Second Front.

In a slightly different compatible terminology, in April 1967 the Under-Secretary of State, Katzenbach, advised that United States–Soviet relations should be considered not only in terms of the evident grounds for *confrontation* but also in terms of the areas of common interests (e.g. re non-proliferation or trade exchange), complementary interests (e.g. space exploration where the Americans could profit by the Russian experience of landing spacecraft on land while the Russians could use the American global tracking system), and compatible interests (e.g. foreign policy conducted within the understood respective spheres of interest of the two Super-Powers).

To sum up, although the distinction between harmony and conflict is of crucial importance, an issue or relationship can as rarely be classified as falling exclusively within one of the two categories as an individual can be classified as entirely good or bad. Our appreciation of the incidence of the two elements in any specific aspect of international politics can be sharpened by elaboration of scalar diagrams, as shown below:

Conflict 100	90	80	70	60	50	40	30	20	10	0	(per cent)
(per cent) 0	10	20	30	40	50	60	70	80	90	100	Harmony

We must, however, bear in mind that in most cases the formulation of suitable quantitative indices for conflict and harmony would involve simplification to a degree that would make the exercise fairly pointless.

3. THEORY OF GAMES

In the stylized classification of conflicts into fights, games, and debates, our interest is naturally aroused about the middle category—if fights are to be avoided and debates are hard to initiate, does progress in conflict resolution lie in the refinement of the games category? Unfortunately, analysis does not offer much promise. We must bear in mind that the 'games' analyse situations in which rational people make choices in rather stylized and unreal conflict situations which aptly apply to games of recreation and chance such as poker, chess, or bridge, but bear only a limited resemblance to real life, whether in business or diplomacy.

The theory of games, like that of probability, is, in its pure form, a branch of mathematics which was first applied to games of chance and only lately to social behaviour. One can readily comprehend why men of affairs become so attracted by the simplicity and clarity of the mathematical structure of the games of chance as a guide to the much more complex social reality. Accomplishment in this theory or, indeed, in one of the games themselves, trains the mind in the methods of thinking eminently suitable for clearly grasping real-life situations. This is so in a very general way but the specific results have not been very satisfying. The first large-scale application to economics through the publi-

cation of *The Theory of Games and Economic Behaviour* by the
mathematicians J. von Neumann and O. Morgenstern in 1944
created a real intellectual stir but its practical results summed up
in *Games and Decisions* by D. Luce and H. Raiffa, which was
published as long ago as 1957, still cover most of the derived
theories. The approach is useful in general terms because, when a
person constructs a situation as a 'game', he has to clarify a scale
of utilities, the range of options among which he can choose, and
the probabilities of outcomes. He must articulate what he wants,
his knowledge as well as its limitations about what the opponent
wants, his scope of choice as well as the constraints under which it
must be exercised. In most situations the player does not fully
know the opponent's capabilities and even less his intentions.
The theory of games helps him to make a more rational estimate
and to limit his choice to the more promising strategies. The
claims of some of the proponents of the theory of games to be able
to provide a full rational guide to decisions, whether commercial
or strategic, has been justifiably criticized as indeterminate, im-
practicable, static, and even irrelevant or preposterous. Just the
same, the impact of the approach upon the way people even quite
vaguely familiar with it structure conflict situations has been influential and, one dare guess, an aid to clear thinking. Although
the actual game theorists may indulge excessively in costly and
generally futile attempts at 'operationalizing' their obstruse theorems and models, the theoreticians not directly committed to the
approach and, it appears, also the American diplomats familiar
with it, seem to profit as it helps to systematize and to clarify their
thinking. Possibly even the barest introduction which can be at-
tempted here can serve this general purpose.

In situations in which the total of the 'pay-offs' is fixed, clearly
the gain of one player must be at the cost of the other. These are
the so-called 'fixed-sum-games'. If all the gains and losses are equal,
as in chess or poker, we speak about a 'zero-sum-game'. Such a
game underlies the starker forms of power politics such as those
distinguished by Machiavelli or generally pursued by the Americans and the Russians in the earlier stages of the Cold War. The
one side's gain is the other side's loss and *vice versa*. Compromise
or accommodation are impossible as they would amount to futile
appeasement. However, even in this situation of stark conflict,
rationality obtains as each player can calculate his probable gains

and losses and find out the most rational strategy which he can adopt on the basis of calculating their chances, at least in the long run. The basis of this calculation is the MINIMAX or MAXIMIN concept. Each player aims at the highest possible gain (which is at the cost of the highest possible loss of the opponent) but will accept the smallest possible gain if he knows that this is likely to be the most that he can obtain. Conversely, if a player cannot avoid losses, he will naturally seek the relatively smallest loss and his opponent will have to limit his expected gain accordingly. If the two players rationally choose 'the worst of the best' and the best of the worst' respectively, a stable solution called a 'saddle-point' is occasionally found. Even if no saddle-points can be found at all, which often happens, a substitute is available in 'mixed strategies' in which each player plays at random two or three of his strategies and, over a long run, both sides obtain the best they respectively can obtain. This analysis proposes what may be regarded as a prudent defensive strategy for the conduct of foreign policy. It offers the best that can be expected against a good player, it protects from avoidable risks, but it requires firmness and perseverance and it offers no chance of quick victory or even of profiting by the opponent's mistakes. The American containment policy is an example; the British policy towards France in the late sixties could be analysed according to this model.

All this analysis does not apply to a single game which has been graphically called 'end of the world' game but to sequences of games, or 'supergames'. This usefully draws our attention to the fact that conflict should not be treated in isolation since it takes place within chains of moves within continuous interactions. Our strategies must not, therefore, be limited to the one encounter but should rationally, and profitably, be designed to profit within whole sequences. Zero-sum-games do not frequently occur in real life; in the majority of situations players not only can win something competitively but frequently they can also collectively alter the pay-off by combining and co-ordinating their actions. This, as well as other statements in this book and in most of the games theory literature on the relationship between the theory and real life, must be taken as a shorthand expression describing the way the real-life parties or we, as their outside observer, interpret and structure the situation. The situation can always be interpreted and structured otherwise, and certainly can develop into a different structure across time. For instance, the French relations with Germany developed from a zero-sum game in the early postwar period, when the French wished—and hoped to be able—to keep the Germans down, into a variable-sum game within the Communities in which co-operation changed the competitive character of the game and rapidly increased the pay-off for both sides. The French gain in security and in economic benefits was matched by the slighter German economic gain to which the benefits of rapid political rehabilitation were added. Until the visit of Mr. Heath to Paris in May 1971, it was not at all clear whether President Pompidou interpreted the French–British relationship concerning the British entry as a basically competitive (zero-sum) or a variable motive (co-operative as well as competitive or variable-sum) game.

Two basic types of the variable-sum games are fundamental. The first is the game of mutual threats graced with the name 'chicken'. Its paradigm is the situation in which two drivers drive fast cars directly at each other and the one who swerves is disgraced as 'chicken', according to the original teenage gang code in which the game was supposed to have been originally evolved, while the winner is acclaimed as a hero; if both continue, they clash; if both swerve simultaneously, neither wins but both avoid disgrace.

Four possible strategies can occur in the abstract model of the 'chicken' situation:

(1) both players may 'co-operate' (CC) by swerving at the same time, saving their lives without incurring disgrace;
(2) both 'defect' (DD) and collide with fatal results;
(3) player A co-operates by swerving while player B goes on and wins (CD);
(4) player B co-operates through swerving while player A goes on and wins (DC).

The four quarters of the pay-off matrix 2 in Diagram IV represent the four possibilities.

The strategic implications are gloomy as there is no rational 'soft' solution even if the game is repeated and further advanced to 'supergame' level based on a whole series. As no rational solution can be found in the game as it stands, it is worth looking beyond its simplified matrix and acknowledging—although it seems impossible to quantify—the value attached by the players to the strategies as such, independently of their outcomes. Here it is possible to hypothesize that double defection would be prevalent in teenage gangs where daring is the order of the day whereas a similar game sometimes played by older men, especially with families, is likely to set greater store on co-operation.

DIAGRAM IV. Some examples of game models.

1. *'Minimax'*
Player B 'Column'

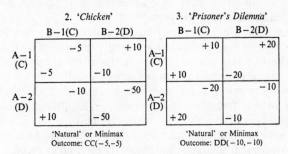

Strategies

		B–1	B–2

Player A 'Row'

A–1: −10 (top), +20 (top); +10 (bottom), −20 (bottom)
A–2: −10 (top), +10 (top); +10 (bottom), −10 (bottom)

Matrix of Outcomes: Each cell represents the outcome that follows if A and B choose the strategies that lead to it.

Payoffs to A are shown in the bottom left-hand corner, and payoffs to B, in the top right-hand corner, of each cell.

'Natural' or Minimax Outcome: A−2,B−2 (−10,10). A−2 is the best which A can do for himself, if B does his worst to him; and B−2 is the best B can do against A's best strategy.

2. *'Chicken'*

	B–1(C)	B–2(D)
A–1 (C)	−5 / −5	+10 / −10
A–2 (D)	−10 / +10	−50 / −50

'Natural' or Minimax Outcome: CC(−5,−5)

3. *'Prisoner's Dilemna'*

	B–1(C)	B–2(D)
A–1 (C)	+10 / +10	+20 / −20
A–2 (D)	−20 / +20	−10 / −10

'Natural' or Minimax Outcome: DD(−10,−10)

(From K. W. Deutsch *The Analysis of International Relations* (1968), p. 119.)

The most interesting and also most realistic game is the one of threats and promises called the 'prisoners' dilemma'. The basic paradigm which has many variants is most dramatically described by a situation in which two prisoners cannot be executed without a confession from at least one. The story runs that the Governor of the prison offers freedom and a cash reward to the prisoner who confesses at least a day before the other does; the latter would then be hanged. If both confess on the same day, they each get ten years in prison.

Again, as each prisoner has available two strategies, either to co-operate (C) or to defect (D), four outcomes are possible as represented in the four quarters of matrix 3 in Diagram IV. The rational strategy for any single game is clear and identical for both prisoners—it is to defect and confess, as the worst outcome here is ten years in prison instead of death in the case of co-operation and refusal to confess; moreover, it is possible to gain freedom and reward. There seems to be no way out and both prisoners will confess and spend ten years in prison instead of going scot-free, as they could. The situation fundamentally changes when we shift to a supergame of a series of plays. Findings at the University of Michigan based upon some 100,000 plays in series of 300 show interesting psychological patterns. Generally the stages were double co-operation in some 50 per cent of the plays in the early parts, followed by a tough competitive period when double co-operation dropped to an average of 27 per cent. In the second half of the series, the competitors (who naturally wish to gain the highest possible scores) usually learn the lesson that cut-throat competition does not pay and, in at least 50 last plays, reaches double co-operation as high as 73 per cent.

Apparently the psychology of outcome is only little governed by the personality of the players but is strongly influenced by the outcome of the first few plays—in international relations Mao Tse-Tung's attitude to both the United States and the Soviet Union comes readily to mind as an example of negative experiences immediately before and after independence. The British efforts to cultivate co-operative relations with the new members of the Commonwealth, despite frequently violent outbreaks of unco-operative behaviours on the part of many of them, is an example of the opposite strategy. Needless to say the actual outcomes of strategies can never be predicted precisely but we can merely guess the degree of their probability.

The game data confirm the political observation that neither martyrs nor cynics do well. The rational strategies which seem to be indicated by the prisoner's dilemma pattern are:

(1) to initate co-operation in the hope that, in the not very long run, it will be reciprocated;

(2) to persist with it as long as it is reciprocated;

(3) to retaliate without fail to repeated or frequent defection by the other party;

(4) to renew from time to time a sequence of two to three co-operative moves to give the adversary the opportunity to shift to a sequence of mutual co-operation;

(5) to remind the adversary constantly of the pay-off matrix since the permanent display of such a matrix during play sequences greatly increases co-operative behaviour.

The general pattern of the game resembles such real-life situations as strikes, revolutions and, in international life, some problems of collective security and of disarmament. The limitations of the simplified game scheme are, however, fairly obvious:

(1) The simple games are limited to two persons; introducing a third and further players complicate the models mathematically and deprive them of simplicity which is their major quality.

(2) In real life, the cost of thinking and taking time over decisions is a crucial element in making calculations, but the game theoreticians have not proved able to incorporate them into their models. Obviously, in the foreign policy of a State which can be conceived as a 'survival game', it is impossible to think of *optimal* strategies and the only possible thing to do is to seek an intermediate or procedural solution. As in chess or in poker, the diplomat can be regarded as a 'good player' if he excels in choosing the most promising candidate-strategies and solutions while a 'bad player' wastes his time on unpromising ones. The costs of looking for the optimum solution are too heavy, often prohibitive, and all we can aspire to do is to 'satisfice' our objectives, i.e. to make sure that we achieve no less than the minimum essential for their satisfaction. This is, of course, no more than the general practice and common sense. The theory of games can, however, assist in it by ensuring systematic analysis.

Finally, I would like to mention an interesting development of the theory by William Riker in *The Theory of Political Coalitions*. (1962) He proposes the structuring of some suitable political situations, primarily in the domestic context, as 'N-person zero-sum' games with side-payments, and advances the hypothesis that such situations create coalitions just large enough in the minds of their founders to score a victory but no larger. Against the intuitive assumption that the tendency is to form coalitions as large and powerful as possible, they are kept down in size in order to limit the number of participants in the spoils of victory. In times of severe conflict, Riker allows, the tendency does not operate as the maximum amount of safety is the dominant need. The model is suited to many levels of United States domestic politics.

In International Politics, Riker's model can structure much of U.N. diplomacy, for example, when a State seeks support for its national position or the problem arises of including States under undesirable regimes in an alliance which means paying the cost, as shown in the attitude of NATO to the Colonels' regime in Greece or to Franco's Spain.

4. THEORY OF BARGAINING[5]

The theory of (international) bargaining is an application of the theory of games to international negotiations or, to put it in the terminology of the theory of games, the analysis of threats and deterrence and of promises in 'mixed-motive-game strategies'. The process can be analysed as consisting of two distinct stages—first of communication, second of developing the theory of a 'fair bargain'. For the purpose of analysis, we can conceive of a spectrum of situations progressing from no communication, through implicit communication, to explicit but not fully trustworthy communication and, finally, to completely trustworthy communication. Naturally, full and perfect information helps, but rational bargaining can take place on the basis of very limited communication.

Among the many suggested procedures proposed to reach a 'fair bargain' which is likely to be acceptable to both sides, J. F. Nash's mathematical one has been frequently quoted.[6] Like most other writers, Nash combines some quite technical rules with a negotiating device which can be useful even when not employing his suggested rules. The rules, as the author admits, are quite arbitrary and could, without difficulty, be replaced by another set of rules. The point about them is that they are impartial to both sides and stated by an outside 'expert' authority in advance of a concrete bargaining situation and are thus useful as an objective and impartial starting point for the process. Their utility is of a similar nature to that of a ready-made code for arbitral procedures laid down in advance which, as in the case of the Permanent Arbitral Tribunal, can be and usually is altered by the parties to a dispute. The importance of having such an impartially set point of reference is generally relevant; if Nash's or anybody else's rules were universally accepted, we would reach the happy situation of easing agreement in a way similar to the simple formulae of fifty-fifty or outright demarcation line along a parallel.

Nash's three technical rules are quite straightforward:

(1) A bargain should be independent of the utility scales adopted by the participants as the zero point in any such scale is arbitrary and should not affect the solution.
(2) If the alternatives and their pay-offs are symmetrical, the division should be equal. If they are not, it presumably must be roughly, though not perhaps fully, proportional to them.
(3) The solution should be 'on the boundary of the bargaining set' so that no point with pay-off better for both parties can be envisaged.

The fourth point is the practical device which is technically called 'extending' the game. An additional pay-off can be introduced, but before being given this additional benefit the parties are required to find a solution to their original conflict. This is a formalized representation of quite a frequent behaviour of a third party interested in the solution of the conflict, e.g. the United States Government offers of a generous capital grant for settling the refugees and for exploiting the Jordan River waters were attempts to extend 'the game' between Israel and the Arabs— in which, however, the parties were expected to find a solution to their conflict first.

The best-known analysis of bargaining is that of Thomas C. Schelling which served as the foundation for other major contributions directly concerned with international bargaining. Using a fair amount of mathematical formulation which he himself later disclaimed as not fully accurate, Schelling analyses a deterrence relationship and the threats involved, using a number of telling comparisons between the behaviour of States and of persons and their groups, especially, without disrespect, that of criminal gangs. The two sides—the 'threatener' and the 'threatenee'—share a common interest in the threat *not* being carried out. According to the relationship between the cost of carrying out the threat and the prize, the situations range between resembling the 'chicken' and the 'prisoner's dilemma' games. As the cost increases, which is the case with the growing menace of nuclear weapons, the *rational* motivation to carry out the threat diminishes. Thus arises the problem of the 'credibility' of the threat the carrying out of which has become irrational. The party affected by the loss of credibility often resorts to the expedient of 'committing' itself, i.e. doing something which makes backing out extremely difficult or impossible. The extreme example is competition for precedence between two drivers crossing an intersection where a total commitment would be too throw away the driving wheel to force the other party to stop. The analogy with binding public declarations, especially the various expedients to improve the credibility of the American deterrent, is quite illuminating, and the concepts evolved by Schelling are now the common currency of their analysis.

Illuminating as it is, Schelling's analysis has been frequently attacked on various scores which have been aptly summed up by K. W. Deutsch under eight headings:

(1) It encourages people 'to think about the unthinkable', making them morally callous.
(2) It has a bias for short-term thinking.
(3) It stresses single encounters or the so-called 'end-of-the-world' games.

Even more important:

(4) Deterrence is based upon the false assumption that the two sides have full control of their behaviour whereas the straining for credibility automatically reduces this control as it often involves 'commitment' to automatic response.
(5) The cumulative nature of risks is not fully taken into account. If Schelling's driver, driving across intersections regardless of other traffic, has, say, a 90 per cent chance of survival at each intersection, the second intersection leaves him with 90 per cent of 90 per cent, i.e. only an 81 per cent chance of survival; after seventy intersections, his statistical chance will drop to one in a thousand.

(6) The assumption that the other side will remain fully rational even under severe stress is rather dubious.

(7) The American writers on deterence implicily assume an asymmetry of reactions—that the others are weaker in their capabilities as well as motivations and that they would be intimidated where the Americans would not.

(8) The most fundamental and damaging assumption is that the motives remain unchanged throughout the play. This assumption is clearly unrealistic for most life situations, especially for politics.

Schelling's general analysis was further elaborated by F. Ikle who worked out a general scheme of analysis for diplomatic negotiations and illustrated it with a great number of examples from international crises, especially Cuba, Suez, and Hungary. Although, to the practitioner, his actual scheme may sound rather too complex and elaborate, the basic insights are firmly based on common sense (the author has been a diplomat himself). Ikle realistically accepts that not all negotiations aim at an agreement and classifies them according to their aims which include, among others, the desire to maintain a good standing, which is, for example, the reason against breaking off disarmament talks however futile they may seem. The negotiation consists of concrete steps determined by the moves of the parties who are free to act as they like. The moves are analysed in the terms defined by Schelling and coupled with 'proposals', i.e. suggestions about the terms of agreement which are likely to be, at least in some measure, acceptable to the other party. The whole analysis is characterized by its flexibility and by the realism of its details. It does not assume that any negotiating situation is immovable but accepts that the criteria of evaluation are constantly changing, although, in any relationship, basic rules of accommodation can be distinguished. One of the most felicitous of the categories is that of 'bargaining reputation' which draws attention to the fact that bargaining is a continuous process, helps us in assessing the probabilities of certain types of behaviour in terms of past performance, and, most importantly, stresses one of the considerations of bargaining which has not been fully treated before.

The latest addition to the major books on the subject, by the Harvard International lawyer Roger Fischer, is the most readable of all and could be readily accepted as the favourite 'compleat

negotiator' treatise. The first major innovation introduced by
Fischer removes one of the besetting sins of previous analyses,
namely the implicitly assumed asymmetry between one's own side
and the other. Fischer stresses that the adversary's internal situation must be fully taken into account and that it is insufficient to
issue threats or declare one's principles and to wait for a counter-
move. Even more fundamental is the second major innovation regarding the utility of threats. Whereas in Schelling's, though less
so in Ikle's analysis, threats are the major elements of negotiations,
Fischer's concern with the internal situation of the adversary inevitably leads him to the conclusion that threats are counterpro-
ductive, as the domestic repercussions on the other side are ad-
verse. Also the statement of one's principles is of little use in negotiations; the prime strategy lies in finding an acceptable proposi-
tion, i.e. one which the other side would find easy to agree with.
Here the author suggests a number of shrewd techniques based
upon experience—for instance, flexibility is improved when the
other side is asked to make a different decision rather than to reverse a previous one which is invariably difficult; and to make com-
pliance easier, demands should be specific rather than general.

7

A Case-Study: Britain and the E.E.C.

1. THE ISSUE

APART from their historical background which goes back to the
Middle Ages and even Antiquity, British relations with Western
Europe since the end of the last War constitute a subject of great
complexity, stretching as they do for over a quarter of a century
and involving practically the whole gamut of political, economic,
strategic, and social affairs. If proof is needed of the difficulties of
analysis and comprehension of these relations, it can be easily
found in the confused way in which the argument has been
conducted during the 1971 debate on the proposed British
entry.

As no general theory of international behaviour exists (see chapter II, section 1) no attempt will be made to present the case-study
coherently, on the basis of one single approach. Some approaches
do, indeed, offer tempting possibilities for such an attempt but
invariably they elucidate only some part of the issue. Thus it
would be possible to analyse British relations with and attitudes
to the E.E.C. from a broad, systemic point of view, centring upon
the place of Britain within the global system and the Western
European and Atlantic sub-systems. It would be likewise possible
to concentrate upon the decision-making approach and to analyse
processes by which the decisions not to participate in the early
phases of integration as well as those to apply for membership
were made, or more specifically the values and perceptions of the
national interest upon which the decisions were based. The relations between Britain and France, or more broadly, between

Britain, France, the United States, and Germany, offer scope for the application of the theories pertaining to States in interaction.

The objective of this book is to explore the utility of theory in general rather than of any single theory; therefore none is adopted but insights and promising approaches are selected from various theories classified in major groups, as in the text, and are applied to the various aspects of the case-study.

A thumb-nail sketch of the story as seen from the British angle may be helpful at the outset. The major periods that can be distinguished in it are:

1945–50 postwar reconstruction;
1950–60 Western European integration without Britain;
1960–63 first British application by the Conservative (Macmillan) government;
1964–70 the Labour (Wilson) Government and the second application;
1970–72 the third application by the Conservative (Heath) Government.

In the aftermath of the 1939–45 War, Britain was involved in Western Europe as never before. Strategically, she kept sizeable forces whose task was to participate in the occupation of Germany, and to ward off a perceived threat from Russia; politically, she was vitally concerned with the possibility of a Communist upheaval in Germany, France, or Italy, and later also with assisting in the rehabilitation of Western Germany; economically, she was involved in the urgent reconstruction tasks. In all these fields Britain shared the same problems both with her Western European neighbours and with the United States. Her position was between the two: as a victor nation emerging from the war with glory and with the tradition of being one of the Big Three, she felt herself closer to the United States, the main purveyor of security and of aid for reconstruction, than to her Continental neighbours, whose status and stability had been gravely damaged by the War. Moreover, the new Labour Government was preoccupied with the building of the Welfare State and with the controversial nationalization at home as well as with the dismantling of the Empire abroad. No wonder they had little interest in Western European integration plans moved by the smaller Continental neighbours and gaining popular support on the Continent. The British attitude was more aloof; it centred upon inter-governmental co-operation first in the field of economics in the Organization for European Economic Co-operation (O.E.E.C.), then in defence in the Dunkirk and Brussels treaties and the North Atlantic Treaty Organization (NATO).

When France became more favourably inclined to integration, largely owing to her need to control the recovery and to contain the possible renewal of a threat from Germany, Britain maintained her aloof attitude. She participated in the Hague 'Congress of Europe' but contributed to the establishment of a loose and powerless Council of Europe instead of a customs and economic union proposed by the French. When, in May 1950, the French Foreign Minister, M. Schuman, made his declaration on the establishment of an European Coal and Steel Community (E.C.S.C.) the British responded negatively and did not join the Community when established.

A major reason for the British non-participation was Schuman's announcement that the Community would be the first step towards a European federation. Britain's objection was political, not economic, and indeed the purely economic treaty of association between Britain and the E.C.S.C. was fully successful. Likewise, she did not participate in further Continental attempts to create additional communities, a European Defence Community (E.D.C.), a Political Community, and an Agricultural Community, but again, when the E.D.C. project failed, she seized the initiative to allow for German rearmament within the looser framework of NATO under Western European Union (W.E.U.) arrangements. For similar reasons Britain did not join in the renewal of European integration efforts in 1957 and in the resulting European Economic Community (E.E.C.) and EURATOM. Again she proposed a Free Trade Association for herself but this time she was rebuffed. Having regained stability and self-confidence and having obtained a range of far-reaching concessions from Germany and the other members of the E.E.C., France, under de Gaulle, was unwilling to dilute the Community through a Free Trade extension. Britain responded by establishing the European Free Trade Association (EFTA) of seven non-members of the E.E.C.

Developments in the late fifties and in 1960 went against British expectations: the E.E.C. flourished while Britain's economy lagged; EFTA proved successful but too small to be decisive; the

Commonwealth ties loosened with the emancipation of further African colonies and the exclusion of South Africa, and although the 'special relationship' with the United States was restored after the disruption through the Suez crisis in 1956, Britain clearly could no longer play an independent world role. Already in 1960 members of the Government made public references to the lost opportunities in Europe. In August 1961 the Prime Minister, Harold Macmillan, decided to apply for admission. The three topics mainly negotiated were the Commonwealth, EFTA, and British agriculture, and the negotiations about them were fairly successful but ultimately failed because the French were justifiably convinced that Britain was determined to perpetuate her traditional overseas trading patterns as well as her political and strategic links with the United States.

The Labour Government elected in October 1964 started with a strong emphasis upon developing the British economy through national planning and upon oceanic links. Their economic failure which ended in a catastrophic deterioration in the balance of payments, led to three closely connected decisions in 1967: to withdraw from East of Suez, to reapply for admission to the E.E.C., and to devalue the pound. The new application to the E.E.C. was not even negotiated; it was vetoed by de Gaulle on the basis that Britain had not yet become fully European in her outlook.

The approach to the E.E.C. by the Conservative Government elected in August 1970 was facilitated by its predecessor's decision not to withdraw the application but to leave it in the table. Being a convinced European, the Prime Minister himself exercised a strong drive while the French veto disappeared with the retirement of President de Gaulle and the increasing difficulties of the French in maintaining the leadership of the Community in the face of growing German economic power and political self-assertion. After a brief negotiation in the first seven months of 1971, mainly about transitional terms, an agreement was reached and, although the Labour Party by an overwhelming majority decided to oppose the entry on the terms negotiated, was accepted by the House of Commons. On 1 January 1973 Britain became a member of the Enlarged Community.

2. SYSTEMIC APPROACHES[1]

When looked upon from the global point of view, the United Kingdom is one of the 150-odd units within the international global system and also a member of several subsystems. It is possible to classify these subsystems into regional and functional groupings. Thus, in general terms, the United Kingdom belongs to the Atlantic as well as the Western European regions and to the non-contiguous Commonwealth. In the field of strategy she is a member of NATO and of the Euro-group within it, and also of the more peripheral SEATO and CENTO. In the field of economics, she belongs to a variety of organizations—EFTA in Western Europe, the Commonwealth, GATT, and a range of economic institutions under the United Nations umbrella. The political subsystems to which Britain belongs are to some extent coterminous with those previously mentioned but include also the United Nations as a whole and the Council of Europe. Obviously any clasification is bound to be untidy; although it may be useful for one purpose, it will prove deficient for others.

If we look at the E.E.C. within this broad context, an obvious initial taxonomic question poses itself: what would be the place of the E.E.C. in relation to other subsystems and to the global system? Analysis is systematized by articulating the independent variables involved. The main actors are the national governments —primarily the British and French ones, but also those of the other members of the Community. The United States plays an important role as an outsider directly involved in the security and economy of Western Europe although not directly in the negotiations; the Soviet Union as the major perceived danger to Western Europe.

The structures (characteristic relationships among the actors) encompass the constitutional arrangements within the Community which can be placed between the extremes of a loose association of sovereign states and the ideal of progression towards some form of formal unity; Britain's changing conceptions of association and then of full membership; relationship with other subsystems in which Britain is or may become a member, e.g. NATO, the Commonwealth or an all-European security system.

The processes are analysed by distinguishing the multiplicity as well as the extension of the scope of instruments (from trade and agriculture to joint financial and economic policy; possible extension to defence and technology, etc). The major alternating modes are bilateral relations between Britain and the single members of the E.E.C., especially France and multilateral ones, the shift of mood in 1970, etc. The major elements of the context can be classified under broader subsystems of an Atlantic political system and of East–West relations.

There is, of course, no end to the number of dependent variables we can investigate, or, to put it more simply, to the questions which we can ask to be answered through developing our categories. To take the important problem of the reasons why Britain had not decided to join the integration movement earlier, we can look into the relationship with the main national actors within the E.E.C., especially France, into the British rejection of the structures proposed by the Community and then loosened by de Gaulle's resistance in 1965, into the intensification and the enrichment of the processes and their improved general tone, into the increasingly more favourable international context with British alignments with the United States and the Commonwealth becoming looser and with the partial strategic withdrawal of the United States from Europe looming large in the immediate future.

The linkage approach offers some useful concepts and develops analytical categories for studying important phenomena: how the British élite perceived the dangers of Britain developing into a 'penetrated' system in which the United States was becoming a potential direct participant in some economic and also political and strategic fields; how the allocation of scarce resources to the rising defence costs made the élite sensitive to the social costs of maintaining a world role and eventually involved part of the public at large. The allied idea of 'adaptive' behaviour offers no promising categories for empirical research but an interesting way of looking at the shift in Britain's foreign policy from her attempts to influence the intractable international environment to an essentially regional orientation and to attempts to maintain adaptation of domestic structures within acceptable limits. This is a promising way for tackling the problems of 'sovereignty' which seems to play a prominent role in the motivations of the more extreme anti-marketeers.

The functionalist thesis and the integration theory offer different insights. It is a historical fact that the majority of the British political élite did not aspire to British participation in Western Europe beyond the traditional patterns of intergovernmental co-operation. It is plausible to argue that the growing scope of transnational transactions between Britain and the Six, not only in trade but also in the widest range of fields from the central problems of common strategy to such peripheral ones as tourism have already resulted in the establishment of a *de facto* political community which will be merely formalized through the British adherence to the E.E.C. While such analysis of integration processes provides a plausible explanation for the past, a stricter analysis of 'integration' as the end-product of the process offers conceptual tools for thinking about the future of an enlarged Community, e.g. in the relationship between 'high' and 'low' politics or the relations of the Community with the outer world. Instead of planning in terms of a simple dichotomy between a loose *Europe des patries* and a fully integrated federal Europe, neither of which is a very probable end result, we can conceive of more complex but also more probable types. Assuming that further authority will be taken from the constituent units, it need not, in Haas's analysis, necessarily be vested in a new regional State, leading to a kind of regional nationalism. It may find no single new focus so that we would be faced with a new type of organization, the 'regional commune'; it is also possible that, through 'asymmetrical overlapping', authority may be distributed among several new centres. The integration theory is likely to provide unique tools not only for understanding the complex process but also for political endeavours to satisfy as far as possible the national interests involved.

3. THE ACTIONS OF STATES[2]

Looking at the issue from the British angle, we can apply Professor Allison's 'rational', 'organizational', and 'bureaucratic' models, bearing in mind his recommendation that each of these has its limited uses but that all the models are likely to be necessary to come nearer to the understanding of the issue as a whole. This distinction can be superimposed upon the decision-making model: the organizational model corresponds with the 'spheres of competence' and partly with 'communication and information':

the 'bureaucratic politics model' applies partly to the latter and partly to 'motivation'; the 'rational' model deals with values and conceptions of 'national interest' which fall within the category of 'motivation'.

To start with the 'organizational' model, the basic complexities of the decision-making machinery involved in the conduct of British foreign policy are not nearly as great as those in the United States system which has served as the starting point for the majority of theoretical analyses. In the case of British relations with Europe the situation is, however, uniquely complex because, apart from the Foreign and Cabinet Offices and the Foreign Secretary and the Prime Minister and the Cabinet as a whole, a host of other departments and their political heads are involved, notably the Treasury which was, in the main, in charge of British relations with the E.E.C. until 1961. The study of the conversion within the various agencies, especially the Treasury, from opposition to advocacy of participation, would be a rewarding task if, and this is a big if, full information were available. Apart from the Official Secrets Act, we are up against the limitations of institutional memory, as the subtle shifts in the minds of influencial individuals could not possibly be fully represented in the relevant files, and many of the main participants are now getting old or are dead. These limitations of information are equally if not even more relevant in preventing the study of the 'communication and information' and 'motivation' sub-categories, although here we can often more fruitfully use the 'rational' and the 'bureaucratic' politics model.

Looking into the information components in the decisions taken, we seek empirical evidence about the incidence and weight of the major inputs—from the international environment, in which Britain's ability to protect her interests and particularly to play a significant world role was rapidly dwindling for interrelated political, economic, and strategic reasons; and from the domestic environment, in which the demands for social welfare and consumption were growing, giving rise to the conviction that joining Western Europe was the most, perhaps the only promising way of meeting these demands. The differences in the timing of the conversion of influential individuals and of whole departments are significant and may be at least partly ascertainable. It may be possible to reconstitute the 'strategic image' or rather the main 'strategic images' of the political élite as a whole as well as of its influential segments and members. If the elements of these images are clearly articulated, we may discover their relative importance in the conversion to Europe which, one may expect, could greatly vary from individual to individual and from institution to institution. Thus we should consider the unsatisfactory performance of domestic economy allied with growing domestic demands, the difficulties with sterling and the balance of payments, the limited capabilities for continuing an extensive strategic role, the changes in the 'special relationship' with the United States and in Commonwealth relations.

It could be illuminating to analyse the contribution of negative elements leading to the decision, such as wrong forecasts and disappointed expectations about the outside world, and of positive elements, such as the understanding and appreciation of the European idea. This analysis can be assisted by endeavouring to analyse the degree of understanding of the issue by ranking it on the axis of high/low understanding and by placing it among other major decisions. A similar exercise could be conducted on the basis of one of the 'consistency theories'. Although obviously our reconstruction cannot be expected to be complete, it seems promising to trace by theoretical analysis and by detailed historical investigation the processes by which the inconsistency between the membership and the ideals of the 'three circles', so obvious to de Gaulle, became psychologically untenable to members of the British élite, and to investigate in particular the role that de Gaulle's determined opposition to the British entry played in these processes.

Modern survey methods and public opinion polls offer a tool of only limited utility. If well conducted, they are reasonable indicators of trends in the past, but at best they offer only an indication of the strength of the attitude but none of its likely permanence. On their basis we cannot forecast with any degree of confidence likely trends and the likely impact of possible future events. A host of surveys and of public opinion polls were conducted regarding British attitudes to the E.E.C.—for several newspapers, the B.B.C., and *Encounter*—during the period May–September 1971. They showed that the general public consisted of a larger group opposed to entry, a smaller supportive group, and of a fairly large undecided group. The majority, however, expected that Britain would enter the E.E.C., as this depended on a parliamentry vote alone. The attitudes of the political élite were much more favourable, as shown in the public opinion poll organized among people listed in *Who's Who* and in the sixty-seven unstructured contributions to *Encounter*. The discrepancy between the political élite and public opinion at large has thus been clearly established. The individual contributions to *Encounter*, although too few to allow for generalizations, enable us at least to formulate hypotheses about the correlations between social attributes and specific positive and negative arguments.

Finally, as Britain's turn to Europe constitutes a fundamental change which requires a rethinking of the basic objectives of foreign policy, an analysis of the changing conceptions of the 'national interest' involved could be fruitful.

To start with, the confusing political statements can be better understood by means of systematic analysis bringing them into meaningful relations with the 'aspirational levels' of the 'national interest' (particularly pronounced with the Opposition and at Party Conferences) and its 'operational level' (more relevant for the Government and within contexts in which an intention to act is signified).

The arguments about Britain joining the E.E.C. can be roughly classified as being within either the economic or the political field, with a degree of overlap. The economists violently disagree in their evaluations of the short-term costs during the transition period, their estimates varying between £70 million and £880 million with the Government White Paper in-between with £442 million. The long-term estimates vary similarly between expectations of great opportunities within a large market and under the impact of new psychological incentives, and gloomy forecasts about Britain running into insuperable balance-of-payments difficulties and becoming an economically backward periphery of Western Europe.

In the political field, the main argument centred around the limitations upon Britain's sovereignty, especially upon the powers of Parliament (with references to the dangers of losing national identity) and the enhanced British influence through participation in the Community decisions. Violent disagreements arose about the impact of the entry upon British relations with the Commonwealth and with the rest of the world.

All these arguments, with varying degrees of emphasis and in perplexingly bewildering combinations, were used in the public debate conducted about the E.E.C. in the first half of 1971. No consensus was reached about any of them and an objective analysis is likely to be limited to a statement that the economic calculations are inconclusive while the political ones indicated that the advantage lay with the entry. Although apprehensions concerning the limitations of Britain's sovereignty and the unpleasant aspects of the bureaucratic procedures of the E.E.C. and of its agricultural policy appealed to many critics, the contrary argument that Britain would, on balance, gain much more in international influence than lose through her membership, prevailed among the majority of the political élite, although not among public opinion at large.

When we try to understand the relationship between the conceptions of the 'national interest' articulated in the public statements and polemics and those applying to national aspirations and to proposals about operational foreign policy, we inevitably enter into the realm of political speculation which, however, can be fruitfully systematized and organized through the use of the analytical categories of 'aspirational' and 'operational' levels. To start with, it is worth stressing that to an overwhelming majority of the participants in the debate, joining the E.E.C. can be most usefully regarded not as a good in itself but rather as an instrumentality to increase Britain's influence in the world and to resolve her economic problems.

The fundamental although inarticulate disagreement between the pro- and the anti-marketeers can be attributed to their different ways in viewing Britain's longe-range interests projected from her historical past and her national tradition. If, as it is plausible to assume, they all aspire to a prosperous and influential Britain, they fundamentally differ in their conceptions of the future. The pro-marketeers foresee an international environment in which a Middle Power will be doomed to a gradual relative shrinking of its economic and political power; participation in a larger unit which carries weight in the world and in which Britain can exercise a considerable influence seems to be the only possible instrumentality for reversing this trend. The anti-marketeers hark back to the past and reject the idea of Britain merging her seperate indentity which would contravene her proud national record and would weaken her traditionally much stronger links with the

English-speaking peoples. To them, a return to a modified but essentially similar past does not seem to be impossible. Apparently these basic attitudes ultimately determine people's stand in the controversy and the various considerations of national interest advanced in the debate are, to a large extent, rationalizations rather than reasons for thinking one way or the other.

Several specific concepts developed in the analysis of 'national interest' are useful. Thus, attention is drawn to the way in which Britain endeavoured to pursue an essentially traditional foreign policy in a fundamentally changed international environment because, aided by varying masking elements (belief in the Commonwealth as a continuation of the Empire, United States economic and strategic support, accumulation of debts), she could merely react to imperious inputs without attempting to rethink the whole of her foreign policy. Not until the end of the fifties did the decision-makers begin to take full notice of the implications of the ending of the Empire, of the permanent military involvement in Europe, of the brittleness of the Commonwealth and of Britain's uncomfortably subordinate position in the relationship with the United States. Only as the delayed result of the devaluation of sterling, the decision to withdraw from East of Suez in 1967, and the new promise of entry into the E.E.C. did the Heath government elected in 1970, begin to rethink the nature and implication of Britain's 'national interest' and use it as a yardstick in evaluating traditional policies.

Analysis of 'national interest' offers interesting ways of looking at the problems arising from the perpetuation of notions developed in different historical contexts, e.g. about the meaning of sovereignty. A major contributory though seldom fully recognized reason for Britain's failure to exercise her opportunities for leadership in Western Europe after the end of the War can be sought in other issues being much more salient—she was preoccupied with domestic issues such as the establishing of the Welfare State and nationalization, and with imperial matters which lie in between the domestic and the foreign fields. Hence her leaders, though anxious to develop the traditional patterns of inter-governmental co-operation, did not have the time or energy or inclination to give much thought to the radical European proposals for fuller integration.

The growing discrepancy between Britain's capabilities and

commitments can be analysed as leading to the gradual redefinition of the 'scope' of her foreign policy. Britain reduced hers just as in a similar fashion the Japanese and the Germans enlarged theirs. Closely allied is an analysis of the spatial dimension of foreign policy as a way of looking at Britain's initial policy of three concentric circles and her gradual decision to concentrate upon Western Europe as by far the most important of the three. The present confusion about the nature of Britain's national interest can be plausibly analysed in terms of the 'contemporaneity of the non-contemporaneous', the persistence of backward-looking traditional definitions and policies and of others which look forward. Finally, among the many dichotomies met and choices to be made, it is worthwhile stressing the importance of a shift of emphasis from political and strategic to economic priorities, the slow, gradual acceptance of the situation in which a Middle Power cannot possibly protect itself by its own efforts and must resort to international co-operation—described in theory as the replacement of 'possession' by 'milieu goals'. Finally, possibly the hardest and most fundamental choice lies in the abandonment of an increasingly powerless autonomy in favour of interdependence which limits sovereignty but extends influence.

4. STATES IN INTERACTION[3]

Conflict research and the theory of games offer powerful intellectual tools for conceptualizing British relations with France which were the most important element in the European negotiations, although attitudes to Germany were probably the more powerful basic background factor. One may think of a transition from an essentially conflict situation to one of gradually increasing co-operation or a gradual *rapprochement* of the conceptions of the respective 'national interests' on both sides which enables the two nations to narrow down the differences between their evaluations of utilities. As Britain set gradually less store upon retaining exclusive oceanic links, France became increasingly interested in British entry in order to balance the rising and increasingly less controllable influence of Germany. With additional though often different benefits accruing to Britain and France from the British entry, the 'zero-sum' game in which one State's gain was conceived to be at the other one's loss is now replaced by the 'non-zero-sum'

variety in which the pay-off is vastly increased by additional
benefits so that all that needs to be done is to agree about their fair
division. This is the field covered by the theory of bargaining,
particularly its analysis of the use of threats. The credibility and
the utility of a purely negative attitude both on the part of the
British and the French Governments are now very much reduced
—it seems most unlikely that France would go to the length of
seriously thwarting Britain's interests within the Community, as
an antagonized Britain could turn to Germany; likewise it is
unlikely that Britain would wish to do that and, even less so, to
fall back on the slender possibility of restoring her 'special
relationship' with the United States.

Glossary of Selected Terms

CAPABILITY
'A State's capacity to effect changes in the international environment in its own interest' (Lerche and Said).

COERCION
'Signifies, in general, the imposition of external regulation and control upon persons, by the threat and use of force and power. Distinctions are commonly drawn between violent and non-violent, physical and non-physical, legitimate and illegitimate forms of coercion' (Daniel Lerner).

CONFLICT
'A struggle over values and claims to scarce status, power, and resources in which the aims of the opponents are to neutralize, injure, or eliminate their rivals' (L. A. Coser).

CRISIS
'Crisis is a situation characterized by high levels of threat, time-pressure, and surprise' (C. F. Herman).

CYBERNETICS
'The systematic study of communication and control in organizations of all kinds' (Karl W. Deutsch).

DECISION
'A conscious choice between two or more alternatives' (Amitai Etzioni).

ÉLITES
'Minorities set apart by their pre-eminence in the distribution of authority, achievement, and research' (S. Keller).

or

'A control unit that specializes in the cybernetic functions of knowledge-processing and decision-making and in the application of power' (Amitai Etzioni).

EQUILIBRIUM
'A state of rest brought about by the interaction of opposing but balancing forces' (Oran R. Young).

FEEDBACK
'A communications network that produces action in response to an input of information, *and includes the results of its own action in the new information by which it modifies its subsequent behaviour*' (Karl W. Deutsch).

FUNCTIONALISM
Postulates that the future can be assured only by gradual expansion of co-operation on broader levels in response to specific needs. Functionalist theory holds that co-operation in technical, economic, and generally non-technical areas will produce a 'spillover' effect eventually undermining and transforming the political form of the nation-state' (Lerche and Said).

FUNCTION/DYSFUNCTION
'... Functional problems are those concerning the conditions of the maintenance and/or development of the interchanges with environing systems, both inputs from them and outputs to them. Functional significance may be determined by the simple criterion of the dysfunctional consequences of failure, deficit or excess of an input to a receiving system, as asphyxiation is the consequence of failure in oxygen input, and so oxygen input is judged to be functionally significant for the organism' (Talcott Parson).

GAMES THEORY
'... the approach of the theory of games is based on the existence of far-reaching similarities between certain conventionally standardized games and certain recurrent social situations. Where such similarities exist, it is held to be more profitable to analyse first the games rather than the far less sharply defined social situations' (Karl W. Deutsch).

PAY OFF
'Pay-offs' are the rewards and penalties scored by the different players, in terms of what seems valuable to them or else in terms of what will permit them to stay in the game'

SADDLE-POINT
The point 'at which the minimum of one player's maxima (i.e. gains) and the maximum of his adversary's minima (i.e. losses) coincide, and which can be attained by (a minimax) ... strategy'.

ZERO-SUM-GAMES
Games in which any game by one or more players must be equal to the loss of one or more rivals.

IMAGE
'An individual's *perceptions* of an object, fact or condition, his *evaluation* of that object, fact or condition in terms of its goodness or badness, friend-

liness or hostility, or value, and the meaning ascribed to, or deduced from, that object fact or condition' (K. J. Holsti).

or

'Organized representation of an object in an individual's cognitive system' (K. W. Boulding).

INFLUENCE
'Denotes whatever causes in any social and especially political context, individuals or groups to deviate from a predicted path of behaviour' (W. W. Ehrmann).

INTEGRATION
Refers *exclusively* to a process that links a given concrete international system with a dimly discernible future concrete system . . .' (Ernst B. Haas).

MISPERCEPTION
Misperception occurs when 'the statesman's *psychological* environment (that is, his image or estimate of the situation, setting or milieu) . . . [does] not correspond to the *operational* environment (in which his decisions are executed)' (Harold and Margaret Sprout).

NATIONAL INTEREST
'If foreign policy is defined as "a formulation of desired outcomes which are intended (or expected) to be consequent upon decisions adopted (or made) by those who have authority (or ability) to commit the machinery of the state and a significant fraction of national resources to that end", "national Interest" describes the desired outcomes' (Joseph Frankel).

PERCEPTION
'Social perception is . . . generally concerned with the effects of social and cultural factors on man's cognitive structuring of his physical and social environment' (Henri Tajfel).

POLITICAL COMMUNITY
'A community which has three kinds of autarkic integrative processes: (1) it has sufficient coercive power to countervail that of any member unit or coalition of them, (2) it has a centre of decision-making that is able to affect significantly the allocation of assets throughout the community; and (3) it is the dominant focus of political loyalty for the large majority of politically active citizens' (Amitai Etzioni).

POWER
'In its most general sense denotes (a) the ability (exercised or not) to produce a certain occurrence of (b) the influence exerted by a man or group, through whatever means, over the conduct of others in intended ways' (J. M. Brown).

PROGRESS
'in industrial societies is identified with increasing manipulative control over the environment' (A. Rapoport).

ROLE
A set of norms and expectations applied to the incumbent of a particular position within a society (K. L. Holsti).

SALIENCE
As a concept, 'salience' '... serves ... to convey the joint qualities of importance prominence urgency and intensity . . .' (Joseph Frankel).

SECURITY
'An ambiguous symbol' (A. Wolfers).

'... a nation is secure to the extent to which it is not in danger of having to sacrifice core values, if it wishes to avoid war, and is able, if challenged, to maintain them by victory in such a war' (W. Lippmann).

'Security is development, and without development there can be no security . . .' (R. McNamara).

SIMULATION
Political simulation 'is a type of model that represents some aspects of politics, (either) some existing, past, or hypothetical system or process . . . the model is always a simplification of total reality, . . . some political features (being) excluded' (Charles F. Hermann).

SOCIAL COMMUNICATION
'Communication is the cement that makes *organisations*. Communication alone enables a group to think together, to see together, and to act together . . .' (Norbert Wiener).

STABILITY
'The tendency of the variables or components of a system to remain within defined and recognizable limits despite the impact of disturbances' (Oran R. Young).

STRATEGIC IMAGE
'The organized representation of the important features of the foreign policy environment' (P. K. Burgess).

SYSTEM, BOUNDARY
'A system is generally thought of as being distinct from its environment or as being self-contained and therefore having observable boundaries' separating the system from the surrounding environment' (William C. Mitchell).

BOUNDARY EXCHANGES—INPUTS/OUTPUTS
'Inputs' and 'Outputs' are the *'exchanges* or *transactions* that cross the boundaries of the political system' from the environment to the system and back again (David Easton).

SYSTEM, INTERNATIONAL
'. . . any collection of independent political entities—tribes, city states, nations, or empires—which interact with considerable frequency and according to regularized processes' (K. J. Holsti).

or

'a special type of "social system", an arrangement created when a number of operating units—individuals or groups—so regularize and pattern their relationships with one another that system-centred behaviour becomes to a large extent predictable' (Lerche and Said).

SYSTEMS, OPEN
'A system interacts with an environment (1) in the sense of receiving inputs and producing outputs, and (2) in the sense of adapting internal structures and processes to the environment' (Oran R. Young).

SYSTEMS, CLOSED
'An isolated system having no significant interaction with an environment' (Oran R. Young).

SUBSYSTEM
'A portion of the whole international system' (C. A. McClelland).

UNION
'A grouping of units able to act in unison on a wide range of matters; less integrated than a community and more integrated than a tribal system' (Amitai Etzioni).

VALUE
'Denotes any subject of any need, attitude or desire' (Howard Becker).

Reading List

ARON, R., *Peace and War*, 1967. A comprehensive philosophical and sociological analysis.

BANKS, A. S. and TEXSOR, R., *A Cross-Polity Survey*, 1963. One of the two leading social data surveys.

BOULDING, K. E., *Conflict and Defense; a General Theory*, 1962.

BURTON, J. W,. *Systems, Diplomacy and Rules*, 1968. Based upon systems analysis.

DEUTSCH, K. W., *Nationalism and Social Communication*, 1953.

——, *Political Community at the International Level*. 1954

——, *Political Integration in the North Atlantic Area*. 1957. Major contributions to the theory of social communication.

——, *The Analysis of International Relations*, 1968. A lucid introduction to international relations.

ETZIONI, A., *Political Unification*. 1965. A contribution to the theory of integration.

FISCHER, R., *Basic Negotiating Strategy*. 1971. The latest contribution to the theory of bargaining.

FORWARD, N., *The Field of Nations*, 1971. A brief introduction to theories of conflict and bargaining.

FRANKEL, J., *International Politics: Conflict and Harmony*. 1969. A non-technical analysis of the role of conflict in international relations.

——, *National Interest*. 1970. Analysis of the place of national interest in foreign policy.

——, *The Making of Foreign Policy*, 1963. A contribution to the decision-making approach.

HAAS, E., *The Uniting of Europe*, 1964.

——, *Beyond the Nation State*. 1964. Major contributions to the functionalist thesis.

HERMAN, C. F., *Crisis in Foreign Policy. A Simulation Analysis.* 1969. An up-to-date introduction to simulation.

HOFFMANN, S. (ed.), *Contemporary Theory in International Relations.* 1961. A clear analysis of the state of theory in the early sixties

IKLE, F. C., *How Nations Negotiate.* 1967. Application of bargaining theory to diplomacy.

KAPLAN, K. (ed.), *New Approaches to International Relations.* 1968. Essays on new developments.

——, *System and Process in International Politics.* 1957. An early classic statement of systems analysis.

KELMAN, H. (ed.), *International Behaviour.* 1965. Introduction to psychological approaches.

KNORR, K. and ROSENAU, J. N. (eds.), *Contending Approaches to International Politics.* 1969.

——, and VERBA, S. (eds.), *The International System: Theoretical Essays.* 1961. Essays on new developments in theory.

LINDBERG, L., *The Political Dynamism of European Integration.* 1963. Contribution to the theory of integration.

MITRANY, D., *A Working Peace System.* 4th ed. 1946. The classic original statement of the functionalist thesis.

MODELSKI, G., *A Theory of Foreign Policy.* 1962.

NICHOLSON, M., *Conflict Analysis.* 1970. A clear brief introduction.

PAGE, A. D., *The Korean Decision.* 1967. The most detailed case-duty based on the decision-making approach.

RAPOPORT, A., *Games, Fights and Debates.* 1960. A readable early statement of theories of conflict.

RICHARDSON, S. F., *Arms and Insecurity.* 1960.

——, *Statistics of Deadly Quarrels.* 1960. Classic mathematical treatment of arms races.

ROSENAU, J. N. (ed)., *International Politics and Foreign Policy*, 1961. A major rev. ed., 1969. Comprehensive reader which covers the whole spread of contemporary international theory without overlap.

——, *Linkage Politics.* 1969. Selection of essays based on the linkage theory.

——, *The Scientific Study of Foreign Policy.* 1971. A major contribution to foreign policy analysis.

ROSENCRANCE, R. N., *Action and Reaction in World Politics.* 1963. Application of systems analysis.

RUSSETT, B. M. and others. *World Handbook of Political and Social Indicators.* 1964. One of the two leading social data surveys.

RUSSETT, S. M., *International Regions and the International System.* 1967. A leading analysis of regionalism.

SCHELLING, T. C., *Strategy and Conflict*. 1963. The classical original statement of the theory of bargaining.

SINGER, J. D., *Quantitative International Politics*. 1969. Essays illustrating the application of quantification.

SNYDER, R. C. and others, *Foreign Policy Decision-Making*. 1962. The classic statement of the decision-making approach.

WRIGHT, Q., *The Study of International Relations*. 1965. An authoritative summary of the earlier approaches.

YOUNG, O. R., *Systems of Political Science*. 1968.

——, *A Systematic Approach to International Politics*. 1968. Detailed presentations of systems analysis.

MAJOR PERIODICALS

American Political Science Review
Conflict and Co-operation
Foreign Policy
International Organization
International Studies Quarterly
Journal of Conflict Resolution
Journal of Peace Research
Orbis
Political Quarterly
World Politics

Notes

CHAPTER 1 (p. 1–4)

1. 'The Art and Science of Politics'; *Encounter* (Jan. 1971). For a somewhat broader treatment of the subject, see Karl W. Deutsch, 'On Political Theory and Political Action', *American Political Science Review*, lxvi (Mar. 1971), pp. 11–27.

2. N. D. Palmer (ed.), *A Design for International Relations Research: Scope, Theory, Methods and Relevance*. Monograph 10, The American Academy of Political and Social Science (Oct. 1970), esp. pp. 294 ff.

3. Cf. the comments of the experienced academic N. D. Palmer in James C. Charlesworth (ed.), *A Design for Political Science: Scope, Objectives and Methods*, Monograph 6, The American Academy of Political and Social Science (Dec. 1966), p. 87.

4. The interpretation of the State Department and of the academic community occasionally produced uniformity of views which can be regarded as disturbing, e.g. on China in the immediate postwar years or on the Soviet Union in the sixties.

5. Palmer (ed.), *A Design for International Relations Research*, p. 303.

6. Throughout this analysis the term is used in its broad meaning, denoting the officials both in the central office and in the missions abroad.

7. Cf. the definition of foreign policy in these terms by Grant Hugo in *Britain in Tomorrow's World* (1969), written with a clear perception of the operation of British diplomacy, apparently gained from the inside.

8. On Prime Ministerial powers, see the accounts of the appeasement, for example, Lord Vansittart, The Mist Procession (1958) or *The Diplomatic Diaries of Oliver Harvey 1937–1940*, ed. John Harvey (1970); on Cabinet powers, Patrick Gordon Walker, *The Cabinet* (1970; 2nd ed., 1972).

9. On the 'linkage approach', see chapter III, section 6.

10. Cf. the model of Allison quoted by Robert E. Neustadt in *Alliance Politics* (1970), pp. 139–40.

11. Cmnd. 4107, 1969.

12. In A. Dulles *The Craft of Intelligence* (1963), p. 302, and J. N. Rosenau (ed.), *International Politics and Foreign Policy* (rev. ed., 1969), p. 245.

13. Cf. the concept of 'dynamic conservatism' in the theory of organization developed by Donald Schon in his Reith Lectures 1970.

14. Paper by Singer and Small in J. D. Singer (ed.), *Quantitative International Relations* (1968).

15. G. Urban, 'A Conversation with G. Lukacs', *Encounter* (Oct. 1971), pp. 331–4.

16. The practitioners' forecasts, although based upon experience rather than theory, are no more successful. Cf. the experience of Lord Carrington (in an interview with L. Martin, *The Listener* (7 Jan. 1971), p. 16) in 1959 when he asked to investigate within the Ministry of Defence the validity of the claim that in no circumstances would the carrier be usable. The analysis of forty-five engagements of the British Forces since 1945 revealed that on no single occasion had the engagement been foreseen. Also the major direction of postwar foreign policy was clearly based upon mistaken forecasts of the evolution of British relations within the 'three grand circles'.

17. K. Knorr and J. N. Rosenau, *Contending Approaches to International Politics* (1969).

Chapter 2 (pp. 15–32)

1. *The Study of International Relations* (1955), p. 498.

2. Cf. J. Frankel, *The Making of Foreign Policy* (1963).

3. In fact there is a degree of conceptual confusion about the very meaning of the term as it denotes both what is going on in the real world and its study. To avoid this confusion I am using capital letters whenever I refer to the latter.

4. My monograph *National Interest* (1970) is a probably premature attempt to open discussion in this direction.

5. Cf. Herbert Kelman, *International Behaviour* (1965), p. 7.

6. 'Trends in International Relations Research', in N. D. Palmer (ed.), *A Design for International Relations Research*, p. 24.

7. Comments of Harold Guetzkov, quoted by Alger, op. cit., p. 27.

8. N. D. Palmer (ed.), *op. cit.*, pp. 83–7.

9. H. Morgenthau's paper in N. D. Palmer (ed.), op. cit., pp. 69, 70. The paper as a whole (pp. 67–71) is a succinct recent restatement of Morgenthau's basic approach.

10. Arthur S. Banks and Robert Textor. *A Cross-Polity Survey* (1963); Bruce M. Russett, Hayward L. Alker Jr., Karl W. Deutsch, and Harold D. Lasswell, *World Handbook of Political and Social Indicators* (1964). For the discussion of issues arising in the use of these data, see Richard L. Meritt and Stein Rokkan (ed.), *Comparing Nations: The Use of Quantitative Data in Cross-National Research* (1965) and Raymond A. Bauer (ed.), *Social Indicators* (1966). See also Rudolf G. Rummell and others, *Dimensions of Nations* (1967).

11. Lewis F. Richardson, *Arms and Insecurity*, and *Statistics of Deadly Quarrels* (1960); Quincy Wright, *A Study of War*, 2 vols. (1942); J. David Singer (ed.), *Quantitative International Politics: Insights and Evidence* (1968).

12. J. D. Singer (ed.), op. cit., pp. 2 ff.

13. In Charlesworth, op. cit., pp. 160 ff.

14. Cf. Harold Guetzkow in Charlesworth, op. cit., pp. 185–91.

15. Cf. N. D. Palmer, *passim*, esp. pp. 292–3.

16. James N. Rosenau (ed.), *International Politics and Foreign Policy*, pp. 573–99.

17. H. Guetzkov (ed.), *Simulation in International Relations* (1963), p. 25.

18. The subsequent account is largely based upon the essay by William C. Coplin, 'The Impact of Simulation upon Theory of International Relations', in A. A. Said (ed.), *Theory of International Relations: The Crisis of Relevance* (1968), in which the relevant literature is quoted.

19. H. A. Simon, 'Theories of Decision-making in Economics', *The American Economic Review* (June 1959), p. 269. J. Frankel, *The Making of Foreign Policy*, pp. 185 ff.

20. 'Lewis F. Richardson's Mathematical Theory of War', *Journal of Conflict Resolution*, i. 3 (1957), 27, 81.

CHAPTER 3 (pp. 32–47)

1. Cf. Oran R. Young, *Systems of Political Science* (1968), and *A Systemic Approach to International Politics* (1968); Morton Kaplan, *System and Process in International Politics* (1957); J. N. Rosenau (ed.), op. cit., pp. 71 ff; R. N. Rosencrance, *Action and Reaction in the World Politics* (1963).

2. H. Lasswell and A. Kaplan, *Power and Society* (1950), ch. v.

3. Under (d) and in section 7.

4. See J. N. Rosenau (ed.), *Linkage Politics* (1969) and, 'Theorising Across Systems: Linkage Politics Revisited', paper delivered at the American Pol. Sc. Assn. Annual Meeting, 1971. For an earlier treatment, see J. W. Burton, *Systems, States, Diplomacy and Rules* (1968).

5. In *Comparative Politics*, ii, 3 (Apr. 1970).

6. See below, pp. 61 ff.

CHAPTER 4 (pp. 48–63)

1. The original, classic statement in David Mitrany, *A Working Peace System* (4th ed., 1946); see also 'The Functional Approach in Theoretical Perspective', *International Affairs* (July 1971); analysis and criticism in I. Claude, Jr., *Swords and Plowshares* (3rd ed., 1964) and P. G. Bock, 'Functionalism and Functional integration', *International Encyclopedia of Social Sciences*.

2. Paul Taylor, 'The Functionalist Approach to the problem of international Order: a Defence', *Political Studies*, xvi. 3 (1968) pp. 393–410.

3. For the opposed views, see Ernst Haas, *The Uniting of Europe* (2nd. ed., 1968) and *Beyond the Nations Slate* (1964), and Stanley Hoffman, 'The Fate of the Nation State', *Daedalus*, Summer 1966; argument summed up by Roger D. Hansen, *World Politics* xxi (1969), pp. 270–1. See also K. W. Deutsch, *Political Unification* (1965); Leon Lindberg and Stuart A. Scheingold (eds.), 'Regional Integration: Theory and Research', *International Organisations*, xxiv. 4 (Autumn 1970).

4. 'International Transactions and Regional Integration', *International Organisations*, xxiv. 4 (Autumn 1970), pp. 732–63.

130   INTERNATIONAL THEORY

5. Cf. Ernst B. Haas, 'The Study of Regional Integration: Reflections on the Joy and Anguish of Pretheorizing, ibid., pp. 607–48.

6. Leon Lindberg: *The Political Dynamics of European Integration* (1963); 'Political Integration as a Multidimensional Phenomenon requiring Multi-variate Measurement', ibid., p. 65.

7. Discussed below pp. 87 ff.

8. E. B. Haas, 'International Integration, the European and the Universal Process,' Macklintock and Burns (eds.), *International Stability* (1967), p. 230.

9. Cf. Professor Deutsch's doubts referred to on p. 44.

10. E. B. Haas, 'The Uniting of Europe and the Uniting of Latin America', *Journal of Common Market Studies* (June 1967), quoted by Hansen, loc. cit.

11. Haas himself later revised his views—see his article in *International Organisation* (Autumn 1970), and their summary in the next section below.

12. *Economic Theory and Underdeveloped Regions* (1957). See Hansen, op. cit.

13. The distinction between 'scope' and 'level' in the discussion of the spill-over mechanism is first made by Phillipe C. Schmitter in 'Three Neo-Functional Hypotheses about International Integration', *International Organisation*, xxiii. 1 (Winter 1969), pp. 161–6.

14. See especially Ronald Inglehart, 'An End to European Integration?' *American Political Science Review*, lxi. 1 (Mar. 1967), pp. 91–105. Inglehart's anaylsis received powerful confirmation from a poll of French opinion con-ducted in 1968; see 'Les Francais et l'unification de l'Europe d'apres in sondage de la SOFRES', *Revue francaise de science politique*, xix. 1 (Feb. 1969), pp. 145–70.

CHAPTER 5 (pp. 64–85)

1. R. C. Snyder, H. W. Bruck, and Burton Sapin, *Foreign Policy Decison-Making* (1962, originally published 1954).

2. H. and M. Sprout, 'Environmental Factors in the Study of International Relations', in Rosenau (ed.), *International Politics and Foreign Policy*, and J. Frankel, *The Making of Foreign Policy* (1963).

3. This happened only recently. In 1962, when preparing for publication my book on the subject I decided to relegate the term to the subtitle as I was dubious whether it would be acceptable to the British reading public.

4. In Snyder *et al.*, op. cit., or Glen D. Paige, *The Korean Decision* (1967).

5. Cf. an elaborate discussion by S. Verba in K. Knorr and S. Verba (eds.), *The International System: Theoretical Essays* (1961), or Rosenau (ed.), op. cit., pp. 217 ff. See also my *The Making of Foreign Policy*, ch. xii.

6. Ibid., chs. xiii–xv.

7. *A Strategy for Decision: Policy Evaluation as a Social Process* (1961); excerpt in Rosenau, op. cit., pp. 207 ff.

8. T. Allison, 'Conceptual Models and the Cuban Missile Crisis', *The American Pol. Science Review* (Sept. 1969), pp. 689–718. The analysis is employed by R. Neustadt, *Alliance Politics* (1970).

9. e.g., Robert Jervis in *World Politics* (1968), pp. 454–79 or in Rosenau, op. cit pp. 239 ff.

10. *Élite Images and Foreign Policy Outcomes—a Study of Norway* (1967). See also my *The Making of Foreign Policy*, pp. 105–10.

11. This section is based upon my monograph *National Interest* (1970) and *The Making of Foreign Policy*, chs. vii–x.

12. J. K. Holsti, 'National Role Conceptions in the Study of Foreign Policy', *International Studies Quarterly* (Sept. 1970), pp. 233–309.

13. David O. Wilkinson, *Comparative Foreign Relations: Framework and Methods* (1969), pp. 6–11.

CHAPTER 6 (pp. 86–104)

1. For recent British books devoted to conflict analysis, see J. Frankel, *International Politics: Conflict and Harmony* (1969 and 1973); M. Nicholson, *Conflict Analysis* (1970); Nigel Forward, *The Field of Nations* (1971). An outstandingly clear treatment of conflict is A. Rapoport, *Fights, Games and Debates* (1960). See also Lewis Coser, *The Function of Social Conflict* (1964), a clear analysis of conflict in general, and K. Waltz, *Man, State and War: a Theoretical Analysis* (1954), one of the theories of the causes of war. Literature on the specific approaches is quoted at the head of subsequent sections.

2. *Discord and Collaboration* (1962).

3. According to some interpretations of Marx which seem to me plausible, even in his millennium of a classless and conflictless communist society, Marx did not think that all conflicts would disappear but merely *class* conflict which would make the remaining ones manageable.

4. Subsequent paragraphs are reproduced from my *International Politics*, pp. 50–2.

5. Basic discussion in Thomas G. Schelling, *The Strategy of Conflict* (1963); Fred C. Ikle, *How Nations Negotiate* (2nd ed., 1967); Roger Fischer, *Basic Negotiating Strategy* (1971).

6. John Nash: 'Two Person Co-operative Games', *Econometrica*, xxi (1963), pp. 128–40, see also Rapoport and Forward, op. cit.

CHAPTER 7 (pp. 105–118)

1. See above, chapters iii–iv.
2. See above, chapter v.
3. See above, chapter v.

Index *

*g. denotes an entry in the glossary, b. one in the bibliography.